REA

Toni Morrison
and the
American Tradition

American University Studies

Series XXIV
American Literature

Vol. 60

PETER LANG
New York • Washington, D.C./Baltimore
Bern • Frankfurt am Main • Berlin • Vienna • Paris

Herbert William Rice

Toni Morrison
and the
American Tradition

A Rhetorical Reading

PETER LANG
New York • Washington, D.C./Baltimore
Bern • Frankfurt am Main • Berlin • Vienna • Paris

Library of Congress Cataloging-in-Publication Data

Rice, Herbert William.
Toni Morrison and the American tradition:
a rhetorical reading/ Herbert William Rice.
p. cm. — (American university studies. Series 24,
American literature; vol. 60)
Includes bibliographical references (p.   ) and index.
1. Morrison, Toni—Criticism and interpretation. 2. Women and literature—
United States—History—20th century. 3. Influence (Literary, artistic, etc.).
4. Afro-American women in literature. 5. Afro-Americans in literature.
6. Narration (Rhetoric). I. Title. II. Series.
PS3563.08749Z83   813'.54—dc20   94-34714
ISBN 0-8204-2679-2 (hardcover)
ISBN 0-8204-4117-1 (paperback)
ISSN 0895-0512

Die Deutsche Bibliothek-CIP-Einheitsaufnahme

Rice, Herbert William:
Toni Morrison and the American tradition: a rhetorical reading/
Herbert William Rice. –New York; Washington, D.C./Baltimore; Bern;
Frankfurt am Main; Berlin; Vienna; Paris: Lang.
(American university studies: Ser. 24, American literature; Vol. 60)
ISBN 0-8204-2679-2 (hardcover)
ISBN 0-8204-4117-1 (paperback)
NE: American university studies/ 24

The paper in this book meets the guidelines for permanence and durability
of the Committee on Production Guidelines for Book Longevity
of the Council of Library Resources.

© 1996, 1998 Peter Lang Publishing, Inc., New York

Printed in the United States of America.

For Ansley, Will, and Matthew

Narrative is radical, creating us
at the very moment it is being created.

> Toni Morrison
> *The Noble Lecture*
> *in Literature, 1993*

Acknowledgements

Every book creates more debts than can comfortably be acknowledged on one page. This one is no different. So here I mention only those people who had a direct impact on what I have done in this project.

I owe much gratitude to Hugh Ruppersburg, the director of my dissertation at the University of Georgia. He was a hard taskmaster, but his insistence on clarity and precision have made me a better writer and a better reader. His skill and insight are reflected on every page of this book. I would also like to thank Heidi Burns at Peter Lang who saw promise in this manuscript and helped me to shape it into its present form. I would also like to thank Christy Desmet at the University of Georgia. She introduced me to Bakhtin at a time when my dissertation was taking shape.

Many people at Shorter College have been helpful to me over the years that I have worked on this project. Thelma Hall created a teaching schedule within which I could write. She and her husband Wilson have always provided me with important insights into American literature. I also owe thanks to Steve Sheeley who late on a Friday afternoon helped me come to an understanding of the Gnostic gospels which Toni Morrison alludes to in *Jazz*. The Professional Development Committee at Shorter provided me with money to defray printing expenses. And Sara Wingard for all of these years has been willing to say what I was thinking but was too

Acknowledgements

shy to put into words. I appreciate her candor.

Harold Newman has helped me in more ways than I can count. He has kept me in the habit of running every morning and in the process has listened to my complaints, stories, groans, and visions. Furthermore, his professional guidance has been something all of us at Shorter could not do without or repay.

Rodney Allen has been my friend and mentor since high school. His integrity and courage continue to be examples to me. What is more, his scholarship has set standards for me.

Finally, none of this would have been possible without the most important people in my life: my wife, Ansley, and my children, Will and Matthew. They have supported me in all of my work, and yet they have also helped me to recognize how unimportant it is in the context of their love. I owe them more than I will ever be able to express or repay.

Contents

ONE

Introduction

Few writers have been more willing to discuss their work than Toni Morrison. Not only has she given readings across the country, patiently answering questions from undergraduates and professors alike, but professional journals and even popular magazines frequently print interviews with her. In these interviews she answers with detail and apparent candor questions that would have gotten from Faulkner a cryptic word or two. These interviews are extremely valuable to Morrison's critics because they reveal a great deal about her thinking. Particularly interesting are her comments concerning her audience. A writer who so willingly communicates with her audience through readings and interviews must be very concerned about her relationship with her readers. However, Morrison's comments concerning audience create more questions than they answer.

In a 1978 interview with Jane Bakerman, Morrison states clearly that she began writing with no audience in mind: "I never planned to be a writer. I was in a place where there was nobody I could talk to and have real conversations with.... So I wrote then, for that reason" (56). Later in the same interview, she states that she keeps no "ideal" group of readers in mind as she writes but considers herself a kind of reader: "I use myself as the Black audience" (59). But later still in the same interview, Morrison

seems to suggest that she seeks a universal audience. Bakerman
asks her about "her responsibilities as a Black writer" and
Morrison responds with ambiguity: "I feel a responsibility to
address—well, I say myself" (59). Then she adds these comments:
"…if you hone in on what you write, it will *be* universal.… If you
start out writing for some people that you're going to have in
mind, it loses something, gets sort of watered down and didac-
tic"(59). Morrison states that she began writing for personal
reasons. Her next statement merges the personal with something
outside the self: the self "as the Black audience." Then finally,
when Bakerman uses the term "Black audience" in her question,
Morrison seems reluctant to agree to such a qualification and
insists on what she calls a universal audience.

In later interviews Morrison seems to contradict some of her
earlier statements to Bakerman. For example, in 1983, Morrison
points out to Rosemarie K. Lester that her focus is universal: "I
don't write women's literature as such. I think it would confine
me" (54). Yet in "an interview essay" with Sandi Russell first
published in 1986, Morrison says, "I write for black women. We
are not addressing the men, as some white female writers do.
Black women writers look at things in an unforgiving/loving way.
They are writing to repossess, re-name, re-own" (46). Once again,
we see the same sort of ambiguity as in the Bakerman interview.

At another point in the Lester interview Morrison states that
she writes "without gender focus.… It happens that what provokes
my imagination as a writer has to do with the culture of black
people" (54). In similar fashion, she has explained, "When I
write, I don't try to translate for white readers.… Dostoevski
wrote for a Russian audience, but we're able to read him. If I'm
specific, and I don't overexplain, then anybody can overhear me"
(Samuels and Hudson-Weems 140). Similarly, Morrison has said
to Claudia Tate, "I feel perfectly qualified to discuss Emily
Dickinson, anybody for that matter, because I assume what Jane

Austen and all those people have to say has something to do with life and being human in the world" (Tate 121). In every one of these cases Morrison seems to insist on the universal dimension of her work and of literature in general. Still, in some respects such a conclusion over-simplifies the matter. Morrison claims that it is "the culture of black people" that "provokes" her imagination. She does not "translate" for the white reader: "anybody can overhear me." But there is a difference between hearing and "overhearing," and choosing not to "translate" could imply that translation may make for easier reading. Thus, despite her use of the term universal, Morrison clearly envisions various audiences who hear in various ways.

These repeated questions and the contradictory answers tell us as much about the literary audience and the interviewers as they do about Morrison's own thinking. These questions imply that the audience can be neatly divided into groups and that a writer may choose to address certain groups and not to address other groups. The questions also assume that certain concerns are universal and others are not. But feminist criticism has taught us that each of our perspectives is limited and that no group of readers is any more "universal" than any other.[1] Thus, how may one distinguish between universal concerns and those that are not universal? Moreover, despite the possibility that writers might direct their work to a particular audience, the reality is that the work will be read and evaluated by people outside of that audience. It is also quite likely that all writers bring to their work influences and ideas that come from outside their race or gender. Thus, we are left with an array of questions. What effect does a writer's work have on people outside of her intended audience? Does it enlarge their understanding of the world, or does it simply confuse them? Moreover, what effect do influences and ideas from outside the writer's perspective have on his or her work? Does it change the nature of the writer or the nature of the work? Sorting out these confusing issues is difficult for both writers and readers: thus the interviewers' questions and Morrison's answers. Nonetheless, these are the very complications that make Morrison's work challenging.

Many of Morrison's statements about her work suggest that she is aware of multiple audiences: in the interviews quoted above she mentions a "Black audience," and an audience of "black women." In the essay "Unspeakable Things Unspoken" she refers to "responding to mainstream 'white' culture" in the opening pages of *Sula* (223). In this same essay, she also suggests that her work has a universal dimension. In other statements, Morrison has described the difficulty of carving out a place for her perspective in a literary culture dominated by preconceived notions of what the audience should be and how the writer should respond to it. In an interview with Nellie McKay, Morrison states that she is "not like" Joyce or Hardy or Faulkner: "My effort is to be like something that has probably only been fully expressed in [black] music" (McKay 1). Jan Stryz confronts this issue in her recent essay, "Inscribing an Origin in *Song of Solomon*." Quoting from LeClair's 1981 interview with Morrison and from Morrison's 1984 essay "Memory, Creation, and Writing," she shows that Morrison sets out to avoid literary allusions because, in Morrison's words, "'I refuse the credentials they bestow'" and "'they are inappropriate to the kind of literature I wish to write'" (31). She also states that Morrison envies writers of earlier centuries who, according to Morrison, "'did not have a critical history to constrain or diminish the writer's imagination'" (31). Such a statement—particularly in light of Morrison's choice of the word "constrain"—suggests that "refusing credentials" is no easy task. Stryz summarizes the dilemma quite well: "With a formal education in literature that concentrated on canonical texts, included a minor in the classics, and culminated in a master's thesis on Faulkner and Woolf,..., she is hardly unfettered by a critical literary history" (31). In her essay, Stryz charts the way in which Morrison "negotiates the obstacles imposed by the task of freeing her own story [*Song of Solomon*] from a literary past" (31). The issues Stryz raises deserve careful scrutiny.

Morrison is aware that a portion of her audience expects her to be like Joyce, Hardy, and Faulkner. Moreover, Morrison knows well the work of Joyce, Hardy, and Faulkner. Thus, her refusal of these "credentials" is very much a conscious act. Moreover, as this study will demonstrate, Morrison's work is not as free of allusions as one might assume from her comments. Furthermore, Morrison is not just negotiating "obstacles," as Stryz states. Instead, she is negotiating among worlds: the world that has known and assumes Joyce, Hardy, and Faulkner—the Western tradition—and the world that exists outside that tradition. Annette Kolodony states in her essay on feminist criticism "Dancing Through the Minefield" that "insofar as we are taught to read, what we engage are not texts but paradigms" (151). In similar fashion, Morrison is suggesting that in some measure she works against the expectations of her audience, the received paradigm. But what form does such negotiation take? If a writer sets out to avoid being "like Joyce, Hardy, and Faulkner," how does he or she signify this difference beyond the mere avoidance of standard allusions? In what sense can such a writer claim for herself a universal focus without invoking a simplistic splitting of the audience? These questions force us to look at the language of the African-American narrative.

In *Figures in Black*, Henry Louis Gates states that "the nineteenth-century quest for literacy and the twentieth-century quest for form became the central, indeed controlling, metaphors (if not mythical matrices) in the Afro-American narrative" (4). Gates bases this statement upon the fact that both literacy and literary form were provinces of white culture. Like all other "white provinces," they were essentially barriers. Blacks could not be considered equal to whites because in most cases, they were

illiterate. Thus, as Gates observes, "from the eighteenth to the
early twentieth century...the subtext of the history of black
letters...[was] this urge to refute the claim that because blacks had
no written traditions they were bearers of an inferior culture"
(*Figures* 25). The refutation was the establishment of a written
tradition—but one that explicitly honors oral culture.

As we move into the twentieth century and even into our own
day, as Gates says, the argument ceases to be one of literacy and
becomes one of form. Harlem Renaissance poets, such as Langston
Hughes and Countee Cullen, approach form in quite distinct ways.
Hughes wrote a form of poetry that not only addressed issues in
the lives of black Americans, but also attempted to explore and
introduce forms that had grown out of African-American culture.
Poems such as "Young Gal's Blues" and "Morning After" clearly
grow out of blues music, not only in their subject matter but also
in their use of repetition and black dialect. Even in more traditional poems, such as "Mother to Son" and "The Negro Speaks of
Rivers," Hughes avoids the language and meter that we associate
with traditional English poetry. Cullen was different. Though his
poetry focused upon African-American life, he consciously chose
to use traditional forms for his verse. "Yet Do I Marvel" is an
English sonnet. Even in a poem such as "Heritage," which
explores African roots, Cullen chooses to use traditional meter,
diction, and rhyme scheme.

We can observe the same kinds of contrasts in Jean Toomer's
Cane, another important work of the Harlem Renaissance. In
poems such as "Cotton Song" and "Song of the Son" Toomer uses
the oral traditions of the spiritual and the work song. In "November Cotton Flower" and "Harvest Song" he uses more mainstream
literary forms—the sonnet and free verse. Toomer's work ultimately moves beyond the stark choices we find in Cullen and
Hughes. He mingles traditional and nontraditional forms in
intriguing ways. For instance, despite its modernist design,

"Harvest Song" echoes the oral refrains of poems such as "Cotton Song" in Part One of *Cane*. Much like Morrison, Toomer quite consciously explores oral forms with a thorough knowledge of so-called traditional literature.[2] Much the same could be said of Zora Neale Hurston's *Their Eyes Were Watching God*. Gates' discussion of that novel in *The Signifying Monkey* explores the ways in which Hurston moves between oral and written forms to produce what he calls "the speakerly text."[3] All of these examples show us negotiation in one form or another: the attempt either to adapt traditional form to non-traditional characters and subjects, or to find new forms for literature that concerns black life.

The issue we have invoked here is a large one, particularly when looked at within the context of the novel as a genre. The novel is by nature a genre that brings together diverse forms and voices. Mikhail Bakhtin defines the novel as "a diversity of speech types (sometimes even a diversity of languages) and a diversity of individual voices, artistically organized" (*Dialogic* 262). According to Bakhtin, the heteroglossia of language is "the indispensable prerequisite for the novel as a genre" (*Dialogic* 263). Moreover, Bakhtin demonstrates that language and intent are inextricably tied: "Therefore the stratification of language...upon entering the novel establishes its own special order within it, and becomes a unique artistic system, which orchestrates the intentional theme of the author" (299). Bakhtin's statement suggests that intent is no simple matter, for it must always be "orchestrated" by language, and language itself exists as many voices. Thus, just as Morrison cannot choose to address one audience, so she cannot be expected to speak one language. Her novels will inevitably reflect the many voices implicit in the American tongue, even though she may choose to emphasize one voice more than another. Bakhtin says that any attempt to limit the novelist to "a single language system" ultimately "distorts the very essence of a stylistics of the novel" (*Dialogic* 265). Thus, the demand that a novelist speak one language or speak to one audience works against the very essence of Morrison's craft.

Not surprisingly, many contemporary approaches to the African-American novel stress the heteroglossia that Bakhtin describes. In her article "Speaking in Tongues: Dialogics, Dialectics, and the Black Woman Writer's Literary Tradition," Mae Gwendolyn Henderson applies Bakhtin's definition to the African-American novel: the "heteroglossia" we find in such novels is comprised of voices that are at once in conflict and not in conflict (20-21). Thus, Henderson emphasizes the complex subjectivity implicit in Bakhtin's definition: the writer speaks a language that is at once his or her own and someone else's, and there is no clear demarcation between the two.[4] Gates sees in African-American literature a confrontation between "two parallel discursive universes: the black American linguistic circle and the white" (45). Moreover, he recognizes in this "confrontation," the inextricable binding together of the two universes: "their relations of identity" as well as "their relations of difference" (45). Both Henderson and Gates recognize in African-American literature an interweaving of confluence and conflict.

The seeming contradictions in the interviews with Morrison and the negotiations that we find in the text of her work become quite revealing in the context of this framework provided by Bakhtin, Henderson, and Gates. Morrison's "discursive universe" is of and apart from the Western traditions in American literature. Morrison herself is the product of the written traditions of Western culture. These written traditions embrace Greek, Roman, English, Euro-American, and African-American traditions, just to mention a few. But she is also the product of oral traditions that reach far back into American, African, and African-American culture. That she consciously attempts to foster these oral traditions is clear from her work and from her statements about her work. But it is also clear that she does this within the context of a very full understanding of these other traditions; otherwise, she could not so consciously seek to avoid them. Since, according to Bakhtin, language to some degree determines intent, the matter becomes quite complex. Morrison participates in and rebels against the languages of her audience. The tension that we find in her work grows not only from the conscious attempt to make a place for a seemingly absent perspective, but also from the fact that the very language she uses is multi-voiced. As Elizabeth Fox-Genovese explained in a recent essay, "To pretend that the story can be separated from the literate culture within which it is told is pure illusion. It exists in the form of its telling, just as the identities of African-American writers exist through their participation in language" (4). Thus, Morrison is apart from and a part of the broad tradition of American letters: this is the tension that we find at the core of her work. As Henderson argues, this tension involves disparity as well as affinity. For Bakhtin, this tension is at the very center of the novel as a genre. Moreover, Morrison has argued that the American tradition itself speaks with many voices.

In "Unspeakable Things Unspoken" and *Playing in the Dark* Morrison demonstrates that American literature is not solely the product of the white male imagination. Even in their absence, African-Americans (and other excluded groups) have created a powerful presence within that tradition. Thus, the tension we find in Morrison's work actually mirrors a tension that exists within the American tradition itself. Fully examining this tension as it is reflected in Morrison's work is the intent of this study. It is an issue that is by nature many-faceted. To what extent does the American tradition reflect broad Western traditions? To what extent does the American tradition reflect the multi-cultural elements that have brought it into being? And most importantly, to what extent does Morrison address and reflect this conflict within her work?

Despite the importance of this issue, it has not been a main concern of Morrison's critics. Nonetheless, the basic direction of that criticism does in many respects underscore its significance. Until quite recently there were relatively few attempts from any vantage point to look at Morrison's work as a whole. Even book-length studies of her work were composed of essays that examined her novels individually or at least from a number of individual perspectives. Aside from the three important collections of critical essays, Nellie McKay's *Critical Essays on Toni Morrison*, Harold Bloom's *Modern Critical Views: Toni Morrison*, and most recently Henry Louis Gates' *Toni Morrison: The Critical Perspective Past and Present*, there were Karla Holloway and Stephanie Demetrako-poulos' *New Dimensions of Spirituality: A Biracial and Bicultural Reading of the Novels of Toni Morrison* and Bessie Jones and Audrey Vincent's *The World of Toni Morrison*. Holloway and Demetrakopoulos present what they call "an honest intersubjectivity" (2), approaching her work from divergent racial and cultural backgrounds and insisting that their differing views provide a fruitful way of understanding the multi-dimensional character of her work (170). Although their readings of her novels are not "bicultural" or "biracial," Jones and Vincent also avoid a unified, coherent approach to her material. They attempt to tie her into a variety of traditions and conventions, ranging from the grotesque to Greek tragedy. Both of these studies emphasize an important feature of Morrison's work: she does not follow a predictable pattern with each of her novels. In fact, to some extent each novel explores new ground as well as new techniques. Thus, both of these studies provide us with an important insight into the multi-dimensional quality of Morrison's work, a matter that will be of importance later in this study. Unfortunately, they do not tie the novels together.

Though the first book-length study of Morrison's work as a coherent body did not appear until 1988, by the early 1980s there were several shorter attempts to explore the novels from a unified perspective. Two of these studies were "Self, Society, and Myth in Toni Morrison's Fiction" by Cynthia Davis and "Eruptions of Funk: Historicizing Toni Morrison" by Susan Willis. In many respects Davis and Willis present the direction that much later Morrison criticism would take. Davis focuses upon three character-istics of Morrison's work that would be important to later critics: the existential quality of the novels, Morrison's interest in naming, and her use of myth and folklore. In tying her work to existential-ism and myth, Davis emphasizes the connections between Morri-son's fiction and mainstream Western culture. Susan Willis, on the other hand, looks at Morrison's work as a rebellion against what she calls "the male dominated bourgeois social model" (41). According to Willis, Morrison's black characters are alienated and fragmented from their cultural roots. This alienation is disrupted occasionally by "eruptions of funk," which she defines as images of the past that cause characters to feel connected to their culture and thereby to feel alive. For example, Jadine experiences such an eruption early in *Tar Baby* when she encounters the black woman in yellow carrying an egg. In many respects her strong reaction to Son is an "eruption of funk." He makes her feel connected to the roots of her culture, a part of her past.

These two essays define just the tension this study will focus upon: those forces in Morrison's work which make her a part of the Western tradition and those forces which separate her from it. Davis' central concerns are reflected in the first full-length study of Morrison's work, the Twayne United States Authors Series book *Toni Morrison*, by Clenora Hudson-Weems and Wilfred D. Samuels. Their approach to Morrison's work is very much in line with the existential perspective of Davis. Davis' emphasis on naming is also a consistent thread in much Morrison criticism.[5] But by far the most frequent approach that Morrison critics use is that of myth and folklore.[6] Three of the full-length studies that have

appeared since 1988, look at her work from the standpoint of
folklore and myth: Terry Otten's *The Crime of Innocence in the
Fiction of Toni Morrison*, Marilyn Sanders Mobley's *Folk Roots
and Mythic Wings in Sarah Orne Jewett and Toni Morrison: The
Cultural Function of Narrative*, and Trudier Harris' *Fiction and
Folklore: The Novels of Toni Morrison*. Arguing that Morrison's
"artistic struggle" is achieving a balance between "a truly black
literature" and a fiction that deals with "universal" issues, Otten
attempts to place her fiction within the structure of the edenic myth
(2). Otten analyzes each of the novels, showing that for Morrison,
the great crime is innocence, for it represents acquiescence to a
corrupt, oppressive system. Moral action in such a world involves
rebellion, which brings about a fall. Only through such a fall can
a character begin to live a meaningful existence (17).

Both Mobley and Harris approach Morrison from a perspective
that is quite different from Otten's, for they emphasize the
importance of the African-American folklore and mythology which
appear in her work. Mobley focuses on what she calls Morrison's
"conscious fictional choices": her use of narrative and storytelling
in order to "recover and reconstruct the past" (17). According to
Mobley, the ultimate purpose of Morrison's work is the transformation of the reader and the culture to which he or she belongs,
a transformation that will "challenge accepted ideas about women,
literature, and commonplace people and places" (17). Harris' focus
is also on the function of storytelling and narrative. After tying
Morrison's use of folklore to that of Ralph Ellison, Harris argues
that Morrison transforms folklore and myth in her novels, rather
than merely "grafting" them onto her work as Ellison does: "We
recognize folkloric patterns in her work, but she consistently
surprises us in the reconceptualization and restructuring of these
patterns" (8). For example, Harris demonstrates that in *Beloved*
Morrison is drawing on traditional folklore about ghosts. But she
also notes that Morrison is adapting this tradition, for Beloved as

a character also grows out of the tradition of the African-American trickster.

These studies underscore issues that are important to our understanding of Morrison. The divergence between Otten's study and the other two reminds us once again that Morrison both rebels against and employs Western traditions in her work. But these studies also underscore for us the important role that myth and folklore play in Morrison's work. Particularly important is Harris' discussion of the mutual transformation of folklore and fiction in Morrison's work. Harris suggests that Morrison is a writer who does not work within traditions; rather, she transforms those traditions.

The other two books on Morrison have much in common with Willis' approach, for in one way or another they examine the novels as a rebellion against mainstream literary culture and society. In *Toni Morrison's Developing Class Consciousness* Dorothea Mbalia provides a Marxist reading. Claiming that her work is the first to show "a direction" in Morrison's work, Mbalia argues that Morrison's ultimate desire is to argue for a kind of collective consciousness for all people of African descent. Mbalia claims to see a kind of pattern in Morrison's novels, and in so doing, she ignores just the quality that Holloway and Demetrakopoulos, and Jones and Vincent emphasize: the vastness of Morrison's vision, the multiplicity of angles from which it can be approached. Such issues are not ignored by Barbara Hill Rigney's feminist reading, *The Voices of Toni Morrison*. Much like Willis, Rigney argues that Morrison represents "an exemption from 'phallocentric law'" (1). She argues that Morrison writes from "outside" literary convention, and she proposes to map this "zone": "through language, through a rendering of history, through a reinscription of identity, and through articulation of female desire" (1). Consciously approaching the work from a thematic perspective rather than a linear one (such as Mbalia's),

Rigney emphasizes the "controlled disorder" and the "serious anarchy" in Morrison's work (5). Moreover, she consciously attempts to look at the work from a perspective that integrates race, gender, and critical theory. The strength of Rigney's study highlights the weakness of Mbalia's: while providing a kind of unified analysis, Rigney emphasizes the way in which Morrison's novels resist such a study. Only an approach that emphasizes the diversity of the novels has any hope of explaining them. As Anthony Hilfer argues in his essay "Critical Indeterminacies in Toni Morrison's Fiction: An Introduction," "Indeed the most convincing essays [on her work] are those that resist critical and ideological closure" (91). As Hilfer points out, Morrison has made similar observations about her own work; in an interview with Nellie McKay, she compares her fiction to jazz where "there may be a long chord, but no final chord" (93).[7]

Curiously, such an observation takes us almost back to where we began, for jazz in all of its indeterminacy is an American art form that owes its being to black culture. Morrison has argued in both *Playing in the Dark* and "Unspeakable Things Unspoken" that traditional American literature is not exclusively white: the studied absence of African-American authors and concerns is in itself a shaping influence. Thus, despite the systematic exclusion of blacks within American culture, according to Morrison, American literature has never been exclusively white. Such a contradiction is very American. Richard Chase begins his study *The American Novel and Its Tradition* with an attempt to distinguish the American novel from the British novel. For him, the distinguishing characteristic of American fiction is its exploration of "the aesthetic possibilities of radical forms of alienation, contradiction, and disorder" (2). In a statement that seems hauntingly close to Bakhtin's characterization of the novel, Chase says that American novels derive "their very being, their energy and their form, from the perception and acceptance not of unities but of radical disunities" (7). In *The Afro-American Novel and Its Tradition*, Bernard Bell argues that ambiguity is one of the defining characteristics of African-American culture and the fiction it produces. Drawing upon W. E. B. Dubois' famous phrase, Bell argues that "a complex double consciousness, socialized ambivalence, and double vision...are a healthful rather than pathological adjustment by blacks to the rigors of the New World" (5). Chase's study examines white writers while Bell's concerns black writers. But they are both studies of American writers. To the degree that these writers share a country, they also share the contradictory, ambiguous experience of racial relations in this country: slavery and its continuing aftermath of oppression. In fact, Morrison insists in *Playing in the Dark* that a fruitful study of nineteenth-century white writers would center around the question of "what racial ideology does to the mind, imagination, and behavior of masters" (12), even dissenting members of the race of the masters: Emerson, Thoreau, Melville, and others.

With such a statement Morrison consciously separates herself from certain aspects of the American tradition. But as Elizabeth Fox-Genovese has argued, complete separation is not possible, for Morrison writes in a language, in a tradition that ties her into American letters. Furthermore, as we have learned, she is aware that the language in which she writes is pervaded always by the expectations of an audience that has traditionally been white. Thus, paradoxically, Morrison writes from a perspective of alienation within a tradition that emphasizes alienation. She writes with no desire to diminish her estrangement; rather she explores it, re-inventing it in each novel, resisting the resolution that a "final chord" would imply. Her novels emphasize tension, not resolution. And yet this tension is her greatest gift to each of us, for it is through this tension that she most clearly ties herself into the American tradition while at the same time transforming entirely our understanding of that tradition.

Notes

1. Two articles that deal in part with this dimension of feminist criticism are Elaine Showalter's "The Feminist Critical Revolution" and Annette Kolodony's "Dancing Through the Minefield." Both appear in the following book:

Elaine Showalter, ed., *The New Feminist Criticism: Essays on Women, Literature, and Theory* (New York: Pantheon, 1985).

2. For a more thorough discussion of this aspect of "Harvest Song," see my article,

"Two Work Songs in *Cane*," *Black American Literature Forum* 23 (Fall 1989): 593-599.

3. Gates finds the tension between oral and written traditions to be a dominant pattern in African-American literature. He traces written traditions back to the African figure of Esu and oral traditions back to the African-American figure of the Signifying Monkey (*The Signifying Monkey* 21-22).

4. Bakhtin defines the "heteroglossia" we find in the novel as "*another's speech in another's language*, serving to express authorial intention but in a refracted way" (*Dialogic* 324).

5. Examples of such articles would include the following:

Paula Rabinowitz, "Naming, Magic, and Documentary: The Subversion of the Narrative in *Song of Solomon, Ceremony*, and *China Men*," *Feminist Re-visions: What Has Been and Might Be*, ed. Vivian Patraka and Louise Tilly (Ann Arbor: Michigan, 1983).

Dorothy H. Lee, "The Quest for Self: Triumph and Failure in the Works of Toni Morrison," *Black Women Writers (1950 - 1980)*, ed. Mari Evans (Garden City, NY: Anchor-Doubleday,

1984).

6. I cannot list all of the articles that take this approach to Morrison's work. These are some of the more important ones:

Craig Werner, "The Briar Patch as Modernist Myth: Morrison, Barthes, and Tar Baby As-Is," *Critical Essays on Toni Morrison,* ed. Nellie McKay (Boston: G. K. Hall, 1988);

Michael Awkward, "'Unruly and Let Loose': Myth, Ideology, and Gender in *Song of Solomon,*" *Callaloo* 13 (Summer 1990): 482-498;

Trudier Harris, "Reconnecting Fragments: Afro-American Folk Tradition in *The Bluest Eye,*" *Critical Essays on Toni Morrison,* ed. Nellie McKay (Boston: G. K. Hall, 1988);

Patricia Magness, "The Knight and the Princess: The Structure of Courtly Love in Toni Morrison's Tar Baby," *The South Atlantic Review* 54 (November 1989): 85-100.

7. The two most recent books on Morrison's work are Patrick Bjork's book *The Novels of Toni Morrison : the Search for Self and Place within the Community* (New York: Peter Lang, 1992) and Karen Carmean's *Toni Morrison's World of Fiction* (New York: Whitston Publishing Company, 1993). Though both are worthy studies, neither of them fits clearly into the two categories into which I have divided Morrison criticism. Bjork's book looks at Morrison's work from the standpoint of the African-American community. Carmean seeks unifying themes in the work. Since neither study is directly related to the approach which I am taking, I have not included them in my critical survey.

TWO

The Bluest Eye:

Reclaiming the Alienated Self

The Bluest Eye begins with three passages from what appears to be a grade school primer. All three passages are identical descriptions of family life:

> Here is the house. It is green and white. It has a red door. It is very pretty. Here is the family. Mother, Father, Dick, and Jane live in the green-and-white house. They are very happy. See Jane. She has a red dress. She wants to play. (7)

The passages differ, however, in punctuation, capitalization, and spacing. The first passage (a portion of which is quoted above) follows all the rules of traditional punctuation, capitalization, and spacing. In the second passage there is no capitalization or punctuation. The last passage contains no punctuation, capitalization, or spacing; what appears on the page is quite literally a chaotic array of letters. This opening is the center of the tension around which Morrison will structure her novel: the distance between the first passage and the others is the distance between order and disorder, between the expected and the unexpected.

The first passage from the primer presents the expected: the pattern that white family life is supposed to take. Juxtaposed to it is the unexpectedness of the other passages. They prepare the reader for the rest of the novel, another jarring contrast to the passage from the primer: the stories of the Breedloves and the MacTeers, two black families trying to survive the Depression. The contrast between the primer passage and the novel is more than the ideal opposing the real or the white opposing the black. It is by nature many-faceted, for the primer is at once the ordering principle of the novel and the form against which the novel rebels. The words of the first primer passage are repeated slavishly in the second and third passages; the transformation in form foreshadows the rebellion we find in the rest of the novel. Despite its rebellion, the novel does not propose a viable alternative to the world of the primer. Thus, Morrison suggests that stories of black life have no predictable form, such as that of the primer. They must be improvised, much like the lives of Cholly or Pauline Breedlove, Pecola's parents. The tension in this novel is not resolved.

This tension here is the result of a rhetorical strategy Morrison uses throughout her work. She embodies the expectations of a traditionally white audience within her novel and then sets up the rest of her story in contrast to those expectations. This embodiment takes different forms in each of the novels. For example, whereas in *The Bluest Eye*, the primer passage embodies white expectations, in *Sula* those expectations are embodied in the citizens from Medallion who visit the Bottom and fail to understand what they see. In *Song of Solomon* the form of the novel itself, the *Bildungsroman*, is the embodiment of white expectation. Each novel presents a new strategy. Morrison thereby forces her readers to look more closely at a world they may have taken for granted. As Morrison has suggested, the unresolved tension in her work is intentional; indeed it is a central component of her strategy.

In his essay "Roadblocks and Relatives: Critical Revision in Toni Morrison's *The Bluest Eye*," Michael Awkward compares this opening passage in *The Bluest Eye* to the traditional opening of the slave narrative: the black voice is introduced by a trustworthy white source (59). In light of such a comparison, Morrison's irony quickly becomes apparent, for the changes in typesetting and the disappearance of punctuation and capitalization and finally spacing make the last two versions of the primer selection nearly unreadable. Such an introduction implies that the family life in this novel may not be understood by a white audience without the guidance of the primer. If lives do not conform to white expectations, then white people cannot read them, cannot even see them. Social expectations are like the rules of punctuation, capitalization, and spacing; without them, apparent chaos ensues. But such a reading may ignore important dimensions of the contrast between the primer and the novel.

Shelley Wong observes in her essay "Transgression as Poesis in *The Bluest Eye*" that the omission of punctuation and capitalization allows "Morrison to break up"—and down—conventional syntactic hierarchies, conventional ways of ordering privated and public narrative" (473). Later in her essay Wong compares the novel to jazz, arguing that Morrison's characters are ultimately improvising order from "the rag tag details of a life" (475). Thus, the issue in this passage may not be merely one of irony but also one of order itself, for the primer sets forth a kind of order that is not only denied by the world the novel describes, but that is destroyed by the second and third printings of the passage from the primer. At the same time, in many respects the novel follows the order set forth by the primer. Morrison introduces each section of her novel with a passage from the primer. It quite literally determines the order in which her characters will be introduced and developed. To explore this issue of order more extensively, we must look more carefully at the characters in the novel and at the narrator.

As the passage from the primer appears to us in varying guises, so Morrison's narrator shifts perspectives throughout the novel. Claudia MacTeer tells the story of Pecola; she imposes a kind of order on the details of Pecola's life, but it is an order that she admits does not work. Despite the fact that the novel moves from Autumn to Winter to Spring to Summer, Claudia's tale ends with death. She tells us on the first page of the novel that marigolds did not spring to life, that they died just as did Pecola's baby. What is more, the narration of the novel shifts between first and third person. The first segment of each section of the novel is narrated by Claudia; she is looking back on events that occurred when she was eleven. The remaining segments of each section are narrated omnisciently, and portions of part three are narrated by Pauline Breedlove. Finally, at the end of the novel the omniscient voice and Claudia's first-person narration merge, suggesting that the voice all along has been hers, improvising and telling a kind of story from the details of Pecola's life.

Claudia's narration imposes a child-like perspective on the narration. The overuse of simple sentences echoes the primer: "Our house is old, cold, and green. At night a kerosene lamp lights one large room. The others are braced in darkness, peopled by roaches and mice. Adults do not talk to us—they give us directions" (12). Several critics have pointed out that *The Bluest Eye* is a parody of a fairy tale. Bessie Jones sees Pecola as "the ugly duckling"; Soaphead Church is the "fairy godmother" (25). Trudier Harris links Pecola to Cinderella ("Reconnecting Fragments" 73). Furthermore, Linda Wagner asserts that the order of details is one a child would choose (193). Finally, enclosing the tale are two perspectives inextricably tied to childhood: the primer version of family life and the seasons of the year reflected in the blooming and fading of flowers.

But Claudia's narration also works against such a perspective, for she is constantly giving to us perceptions far beyond the capabilities of a child. Despite her overuse of simple sentences, she gives us an adult's description of her illness in segment one of

"Autumn": "I cough once, loudly, through bronchial tubes already packed tight with phlegm" (13). Furthermore, even Claudia's introduction to the novel is saturated with a kind of judgment that goes far beyond that of a child. Speaking in retrospect, she tells us that her innocence is dead and that the marigolds failed to bloom because the earth itself was "unyielding" (9). Such a judgment is vital to our understanding of the novel, for when we place it into the context of the society that the novel describes, it suggests that the world in which the Breedloves live is in part responsible for their condition. Claudia tells us that seeds fail to grow in soil that does not yield. She implies that the same charge could be brought against the society that the Breedloves inhabit: it has no room for any pattern that does not follow the primer. Such observations, such figurations are far beyond the powers of a child. Finally, Claudia's narration has about it a kind of tenuousness: "But was it really like that? As painful as I remember? Only mildly" (14). Later she says, "But my memory is uncertain" (146). She is unsure of the accuracy of her story.

We must also place Claudia's narration into the context of the omniscient perspective we find throughout the novel. If the omniscient voice is Claudia's, we again find a kind of incongruity. Though Claudia frequently gives us information beyond the perspective of a child, she does confine herself to the here and now. There is no attempt on her part to enter the minds or houses of other characters. The omniscient narrator moves freely, first into houses—those of the Breedloves in "Autumn," of Geraldine in "Winter"—then into minds and lives—those of Pauline and Cholly Breedlove in "Spring," of Soaphead Church in "Summer." The effect is very much as Wong asserts—a kind of jazz. Morrison presents us with a story improvised from memory, judgment, and omniscient forays into the minds, lives, and settings of characters beyond the self. But these forays are forced once again into the perspective of the self, the self of an adult/child coming to terms with life, judging it. In fact, Lynne Tirrell argues that the main difference between Claudia and Pecola is the story that Claudia tells, for in telling such a story she becomes a moral agent, a source of judgment. Pecola is the reverse: a passive victim (121).

Discrepancy is thus apparent throughout the story. There is a discrepancy between the primer version of reality and the reality of black life presented in the novel, and there is discrepancy within the narration of the novel. But these discrepancies have to do with the telling of the story. There is also a kind of discrepancy within the characters in the story. The main characters spring from cultures that are in many respects whole and vital, but because of their orphanhood and their rootlessness, they are unable to use these cultures as sustaining forces in their lives. The result is a search for freedom in one case and a flight from it in the other.

Both Pauline and Cholly are transplanted southerners. In fact, much of the background information that the novel offers about them concerns their connections to Southern culture and their migration north. Still, both Cholly and Pauline are essentially orphans. They bring little of their past with them when they come north. In this respect, they support Marilyn Mobley's contention that Morrison's novels are "a response to the loss of tradition, ways of knowing and ways of perceiving oneself and the world" (95). Morrison describes in great detail the "loss of tradition" in the lives of Pauline and Cholly. Though Pauline's parents do not desert her, they display no real interest in her. The narrator tells us that the only fact that saves her from anonymity within the family is her injured foot, which, because it is neglected, leaves her with a limp. She has no nickname within the family, and there are no fond stories about her past. Originally from Alabama, her family migrates northward to Kentucky where she meets Cholly. Together, she and Cholly complete the migration north, settling in Lorain, Ohio. In the present time of the story, they are cut off psychologically and physically from their past.

Cholly's family is completely unconcerned with him. His mother deserts him on a junk heap by the railroad track when he is four days old. When at fourteen he finds his father, Cholly receives no recognition from him. The sustaining force in his early life is his Great Aunt Jimmy, whose presence gives a real sense of tradition and community in the novel. According to Trudier Harris, folk traditions form a "backdrop" in *The Bluest Eye* ("Reconnecting" 68). Aunt Jimmy is a major part of this backdrop. Not only does she care for Cholly as if he were her own, in the manner of a traditional parent, but also as Harris points out, she embodies Southern black culture: the asafetida bag she wears around her neck, her purple head rag, the collards she eats--all of these reflect the customs of her ancestors ("Reconnecting" 69). The same can be said of Blue Jack, the drayman Cholly rides with in his job at Tyson's Feed and Grain Store. He tells Cholly "old timey stories.... How the black people hollered, cried, and sang" (106). Finally, Harris argues that Morrison uses the sickness, death, and burial of Aunt Jimmy to demonstrate community traditions in action ("Reconnecting" 70). Aunt Jimmy's sickness is diagnosed by M'Dear, a community woman who is "a competent midwife and decisive diagnostician" (108). Her very being exudes the power of community and tradition. Thus, whether M'Dear's diagnosis is right or wrong, its effect on the community is immediate. All of the women around Aunt Jimmy follow M'Dear's instructions and bring Aunt Jimmy pot liquor to drink: the words of M'Dear are a call to communal action. The funeral is also a community event. Cholly is treated with the same attention that Aunt Jimmy received in her sickness: "Cholly was the major figure, because he was 'Jimmy's boy, the last thing she loved,' and 'the one who found her'" (111).

Importantly, when Cholly leaves the South, he does not bring any of these traditions or people with him. The narrator makes this clear: "With no more thought than a chick leaving its shell, he stepped off the porch" (120). Thus, Cholly becomes like so much else in this novel: an emblem of disintegration. And the narrator's description of him brings us back to Wong's description of this novel as a kind of jazz: "The pieces of Cholly's life could become coherent only in the head of a musician" (125). But it is a particular quality of jazz that Morrison wants us to think of in relation to Cholly: its lack of final form. As the narrator explains, "Only a musician would sense, know, without even knowing that he knew, that Cholly was free. Dangerously free. Free to feel whatever he felt—fear, guilt, shame, love, grief, pity. Free to be tender or violent, to whistle or weep" (125). This statement brings to mind the formlessness of improvisational jazz, a music that is quite literally free to go where the musician wants to take it. This statement reminds us of the narration of the novel which in some respects is also improvisational: in some places it is first person; in others it is omniscient.

If Cholly chooses freedom, Pauline chooses the opposite—subjugation. But Morrison makes it clear that these choices are not complete opposites. Initially, Pauline is like Cholly: she has no coherent sense of the past. When describing her first meeting with Cholly, Pauline talks of color, much as the narrator talks of sound in relation to Cholly. After saying that she could feel the purple of berries, the yellow of lemonade, and green of june bugs inside her, she says that Cholly brought all of those colors together for her: "*So when Cholly come up and tickled my foot, it was like them berries, that lemonade, them streaks of green the june bugs made, all come together*" (92). Since each of these colors is connected to her past in the South, Cholly's fusion of them brings to Pauline a kind of wholeness. Just as the imagined musician would make the pieces of Cholly's life "coherent," so Cholly brings coherence to Pauline. But it is a coherence that cannot survive the move north. In the North Pauline says there are no june bugs, white people "*was everywhere*," and black people were "*dicty like*" (93). In a poignant description of her estrangement (and an allusion to the primer), Pauline says "*I didn't even have a cat to talk to*" (93).

Pauline chooses servitude as a way of coping with the North. First, she goes to the movies. Watching them, she becomes convinced of her own ugliness. Next, she goes to church. But her choice of churches does not reflect the community traditions that Aunt Jimmy's funeral shows us. Rather than being inclusive, Pauline's church is exclusive. It is a church "where shouting was frowned upon," where Pauline could be "outraged by painted ladies who thought only of clothes and men" (100). There her subjugation finds form: "Holding Cholly as a model of sin and failure, she bore him like a crown of thorns and her children like a cross" (100). In the final phase of her enslavement Pauline becomes the "ideal servant." Working in the neatly kept home of the Fishers, she finally finds the nickname she was denied as a child. She becomes Polly and devotes herself to order: "Here she could arrange things, clean things, line things up in neat rows" (101).

Cholly's freedom contrasts sharply to Pauline's subjugation. Her cultivation of order and respectability contrasts with his slovenly drunkenness and his incestuous relationship with Pecola. But both patterns of behavior are expressions of the same fragmentation that the novel as a whole focuses upon. In fact, the difference between Cholly and Pauline mirrors the tension between the passages from the primer. Pauline's life is tightly structured, just like the first primer version of reality. Cholly's life has no final form, much like the last two versions of the primer passage.

Such an observation is not new. Many critics have noted the basic contrast in Morrison's work between those characters who live in the context of chaos and those who demand from life rigid order. In her essay "Artists and the Art of Living: Order and Disorder in Toni Morrison's Fiction," Elizabeth House argues that Morrison uses such a contrast to suggest that life and art demand a balance of chaos and order (43-44). Morrison's characters often fail to find such a balance. And in many respects balance is absent from this novel.

It is tempting to seek such a balance in Claudia, the narrator, the creator of this story. If we can find such a balance in her, then we can assume that she at least is able to impose a kind of order on the chaos of the lives of the Breedloves. Claudia's family certainly grants to her the kind of love and support that Pecola does not find in her family. Claudia describes her mother's ministrations to her during her sickness in unequivocal terms: "Love, thick and dark as Alaga syrup, eased up into that cracked window" (14). When Mr. Henry tries to molest Frieda, Mr. MacTeer throws a tricycle at him and Mrs. MacTeer hits him with a broom. At another point in the story, Claudia describes her father in these terms: "Wolf killer turned hawk fighter, he worked night and day to keep one from the door and the other from under the windowsills" (52). All of these events throw into sharp relief the actions of the Breedloves. Mrs. Breedlove abandons Pecola for the Fisher's child when Pecola visits her at work. Furthermore, Cholly never provides his family with a stable home: early in the novel, Claudia notes that the Breedloves are "being put *out*doors" (18). And finally, rather than protecting Pecola as Mr. MacTeer does Claudia, Cholly Breedlove rapes her.

Still, despite the stability of her background, Claudia is never satisfied with her relationship with Pecola or with her telling of Pecola's story. Claudia conveys this in numerous passages. We have discussed the shifting from first person to omniscient point of view. Also, the cycle of nature that serves as a structure (an order) for the story does not truly reflect Pecola's development: she is raped in "Spring"; in "Summer" her baby dies. But most importantly, late in the book, when omniscient and first-person narrators come together, Claudia herself tells us of her failure. In that passage, we recognize that Pecola, supposedly the center of the narrative, is someone Claudia scarcely knows. Claudia tells us "We saw her sometimes" (158), but she later qualifies this with another statement: "We tried to see her without looking at her" (158).Then finally, she says "So we avoided Pecola Breedlove —forever" (158). The next line of the passage puts Pecola beyond our reach in an image that emphasizes obscurity: "And the years folded up like pocket handkerchiefs" (159). Next the narrator judges her own behavior toward Pecola and finds in herself the same attitude she has seen in the town: "All of us—all who knew her—felt so wholesome after we cleaned ourselves on her" (159). Thus, though Claudia sets out to tell the story of Pecola and her search for blue eyes, ultimately she separates herself from Pecola, abandoning her just as everyone else has done. And like everyone else, Claudia uses Pecola as a scapegoat.

At other points, Claudia questions her telling of the story. She says, "Her [Pecola's] inarticulateness made us believe we were eloquent....we rearranged lies and called it truth" (159). Finally, Pecola is a bird who cannot fly, "her head jerking to the beat of a drummer so distant only she could hear.... Beating the air, a winged but grounded bird intent on the blue void it could not reach—could not even see—but which filled the valleys of the mind" (158). Pecola's plight becomes in the narrator's telling of it something we can only glimpse. Thus, we are returned to the contrast at the beginning of the book. If the primer version of reality presents us with an ideal that is incompatible with real life, in particular black life, then we might expect this novel to present us with an alternative. Instead, it deals at its center with a kind of inarticulateness, an attempt to say something that the narrator suggests has not been said. As Claudia's statement shows us, Pecola's very inability to speak convinces Claudia of her own ability to speak for Pecola. But in the end Claudia realizes that she too lacks the articulation needed to tell this story. Thus, the discrepancies we have discussed in the narration and the characters of this story lead somewhere. This is a story that finally cannot be put together.

Morrison has emphasized the difficulty of writing about black culture in a world that has been slow to accept or understand such writing ("Unspeakable" 223). This novel becomes a reflection of that difficulty. Claudia summarizes her story in the epilogue: "A little black girl yearns for the blue eyes of a little white girl, and the horror at the heart of her yearning is exceeded only by the evil of fulfillment" (158). It is the "horror" and the "evil" with which this novel attempts to deal; but ultimately as Claudia tells us, she can only approach the subject without ever fully confronting it. It is a novel that explains by not explaining.

Morrison has said that she wrote this novel in part because of the scarcity of books that realistically addressed black life: "I wanted to write the kind of book that I wanted to read" (Bakerman 59). She has also said that she wanted to suggest that the problems of black life could not be solved by simplistic "Black is Beautiful" rhetoric (Harris, *Fiction and Folklore* 17). But in some respects, her project failed: "The shattered world I built (to complement what is happening to Pecola)..., does not in its present form handle effectively the silence at its center" (Morrison, "Unspeakable" 220). The silence at the center of this novel is Pecola. She cannot speak for herself, nor can Claudia speak for her. Still, the very form of the failure gives us important insight into the central subject of this study: negotiation.

Trudier Harris has compared this novel to *The Waste Land* (*Fiction and Folklore* 27). There are clearly some similarities. Morrison's use of contrasts echoes Eliot: spring comes and Pecola is raped; summer comes and her baby dies. But the differences between these works are more important than the similarities. The cultural breakdown that Eliot describes grows in part out of a failure by the modern world to understand structures of meaning from the past. The "young man carbuncular" who seduces the typist in "The Fire Sermon" is "One of the low on whom assurance sits/ As a silk hat on a Bradford millionaire" (44). Eliot's simile directly connects the meaninglessness of this young man's sexuality to his lack of a past: a "Bradford millionaire" is new money. This point is emphasized by the narrator Eliot chooses for this section of "The Fire Sermon." Being a figure from the ancient world, Tiresias represents all of those structures that the modern world has lost. He is quite literally one of those "withered stumps of time" (40) that Eliot's narrator refers to in "A Game of Chess." Tiresias foretells the seduction of the typist just as he foretold the fall of Oedipus, but in the world of *The Waste Land* his presence is surreal. He cannot argue with the characters before him as he did with Oedipus. He can only witness the meaninglessness of their actions, actions that are never regretted in the way that Oedipus regrets his failings. But the world that Tiresias represents is a world that does not have a place for Pecola and Claudia. African or African-American myths have no role in *The Waste Land*, nor do black characters. The aridity of the world Pecola and Claudia inhabit has been engendered by the insistence upon a particular kind of order: that order provided by the white world. Such an insistence renders other structures as unintelligible as letters without punctuation or spacing. Thus, all the important characters seek something from the primer, or they find themselves like Cholly—"Dangerously free" (125). Pecola seeks blue eyes. Mrs. Breedlove seeks an image of herself as Jean Harlow (97) or as an orderly white housewife (101). Cholly rebels against the white culture represented by the primer, but his rebellion takes him nowhere. He kills three white men, and he is free of any code of morality, white or black. But in his freedom he succeeds only in turning the world upside down: rape becomes in his eyes an expression of love.

At the end of the novel Claudia explains Cholly's actions. It is she who tells us that Cholly loved Pecola (159). Her understanding is fitting; she too has experienced the fruitlessness of rebellion. Earlier in the novel she describes her hatred of the white dolls her friends loved. She destroyed them and imagined doing the same things to white children, all in an attempt to understand the "mystery": "the secret of the magic they weaved on others" (22). But the violence she imagines is "disinterested" and it gives way to a "fraudulent love" for Shirley Temple that complements the "fraudulent hatred" she felt earlier (22). All of these emotions are "fraudulent" because they all find their source in the primer. They are reactions to white culture, and whether acts of conformity or rebellion, they are still reactions. They posit no original conception of the self or of the culture in which the Breedloves and the MacTeers live.

Claudia begins this novel by confessing her limitations. "Why" is difficult to explain; she will tell us only "how" (9). In this statement, she admits her inability to face the central problem of *The Bluest Eye*: the monolithic nature of white cultural expectations. In its shadow she crafts a story, improvises a fiction that gives us glimpses of Pecola, Cholly, Mrs. Breedlove, and of Claudia too. But she is no more able to pierce the heart of their mystery than she is the mystery of the white baby doll. Thus, ultimately the "silence" at the core of this novel is the product of two mysteries: the one at the heart of the Breedloves and the one at the heart of the white doll, which comes to stand for the cultural expectations of the primer. Ultimately, though Claudia gives us chilling insights, she too is unable to go beyond the primer. It literally provides her with a way to organize her story: she begins with houses and ends with friends, just as the primer does. Moreover, alternate sections of the story (those told by the omniscient narrator) begin with passages from the primer. Thus, the tension in this novel is expressed most clearly by the narrator. The story she tells both underscores and undercuts the orderliness of the primer.

Early in the novel, Claudia describes in detail her attempt to destroy white baby dolls. After she describes destroying the body of the doll, she gets to the part of the doll that makes it talk: "I could see the disk with six holes, the secret of the sound. A mere metal roundness" (21). The machine-like center of the doll is as close as we get to solving the mystery of its appeal, just as Pecola's "head jerking" is as close as we get to the core of her mystery. Between these extremes is the novel itself: an attempt to tell a story that has not been told, a beginning tense with silence. But as a beginning it shatters for us the superficial order that the primer presents, suggesting that reality has no such neat demarcations. It also shatters for us the coherent narration that we expect of novels. This novel is improvisational because it has to be: only through such an approach can we begin to understand the fractured reality it attempts to describe.

Like Cholly's life, *The Bluest Eye* is a series of pieces that can only be put together improvisationally. There is no set order. In this regard the novel is like improvisational jazz. By playing without written music, key signature, or time signature, the musician creates a world that is always in the process of becoming. It is constantly moving from an infinitude of possible notes to those he actually plays. Such is the order and lack of order that Morrison insists upon. It is an order that does not explain so much as it destroys the explanation presented by the primer. Paradoxically, at the same time, it relies upon the primer for its order. Thereby, Morrison suggests that there is no other order, only the fraudulent one provided by the primer.

By questioning the order of the primer, Morrison ties her novel into a tradition of dissent identified by Bakhtin. Katarina Clark and Michael Holquist argue that for Bakhtin the history of the novel was "a long contest between two stylistic lines of development." Though Bakhtin never defined these two lines, Clark and Holquist argue persuasively that they might be called the "monoglot" and the "heteroglot," meaning one voice and many voices. The central characteristic of the "heteroglot" line of development is its "attack on literary and other monologizing, 'refined' languages" (291 - 292). Such a definition would certainly apply to *The Bluest Eye*, for this novel breaks "up—and down" (as Wong asserts) the order presented by the primer, the single voice of the white baby doll. In so doing, it is for Morrison a beginning, an attempt to talk about what has not been talked about before. Such a novel places Morrison squarely in the tradition of dissent that Richard Chase identifies in the American novel. In fact, the experimental nature of *The Bluest Eye* is a familiar pattern in classic American novels such as *Moby Dick*. Chase calls *Moby Dick* "one of the most audacious [hybrids]..., that have ever been conceived." Then he quotes Melville's famous statement, "'I try everything, I achieve what I can.'" (100). We can hear a haunting echo of Melville's statement in what Morrison says about there being a "silence" at the center of her novel: she too achieves what she can. But again there is a distinction between Morrison's work and traditional American literature. According to Chase, Melville's concerns in *Moby Dick* are very much the concerns of most American novelists: "Solipsism, hypnotic self-regard, and imprisonment within the self" (107). The last of these issues is also a concern in *The Bluest Eye*. But the imprisonment that Chase refers to grows out of a culture where, according to Tocqueville, "'each citizen is habitually engaged in the contemplation of a very puny object: namely himself'" (Chase 8).[1] Ahab is imprisoned by a desire to know the unknowable, a desire to destroy that force in nature that has imposed itself upon him. But he is free to think of himself in any way he wishes, even to the point of envisioning a whole crew of men acting out his diabolical search for the brute animal who took his leg. Morrison's characters do not have the freedom to contemplate themselves, for civilization has defined them as alien. Thereby, it has limited their freedom, transforming how they may contemplate themselves. They must desperately seek the pattern for their lives in the primer, as Mrs. Breedlove and Pecola do, or they will find themselves without form, as Cholly does. Thus, the self-absorption that Melville explores is something not possible for these characters, for they find the self they inhabit previously defined, discarded, rejected—known by neither Tiresias or the grade-school primer.

The freedom to contemplate the self, to tell again and again the story of its alienation and imprisonment, is one that American writers from Cooper to Faulkner to Updike have taken for granted. But Morrison suggests that such freedom may not exist for the black writer. This novel begins with the primer version of reality because it is inescapable. Thus, the issue becomes not escape but reconciliation, not with the society that has disinherited them but with the self that has been disinherited.

Notes

1. Morrison takes issue with this very point in *Playing in the Dark*: "What, one wants to ask, are Americans alienated from? What are Americans so insistently innocent of? Different from?" (45). According to Morrison, each of these traits is predicated upon the existence of a slave population. Only a group of people who could not choose alienation, innocence, or difference could enable the white settler to make such claims.

THREE

Sula:

Of Time and Communities

Morrison radically alters her focus in *Sula*. *The Bluest Eye* begins with an idealized portrait of white family life. *Sula* opens with a realistic portrait of black town life. The opening of *The Bluest Eye* presents black culture through the prism of white expectations. The opening of *Sula* reverses this pattern, for in the prologue to *Sula*, white characters are looking at black town life without comprehension. Also, in place of the passage from the primer, which presents the white ideal in *The Bluest Eye*, there is a fable-like account of the origin of the Bottom, the black community. Most importantly, in *Sula* Morrison defies reader expectation by rapidly shifting the focal points. As in *The Bluest Eye*, the reader is asked to put together a contrasting array of characters and places: Sula and Nel, Helene and Eva, the Bottom and Medallion. Much like the world of the Breedloves, the Bottom is hard for the white reader to understand because it does not conform to traditional norms and values, but it does have its own kind of order.[1]

The difficulties of *The Bluest Eye* are the result of Claudia's attempt to tell the story that she finally confesses she cannot tell. The difficulties in *Sula* have quite a different source. The order that prevails in the Bottom embraces opposites, diversity; consequently, it is foreign to white, middle-class culture. For that reason the novel opens with those blank, uncomprehending stares of the citizens of

Medallion as they watch the behavior of Bottom citizens. Thus, whereas Morrison focuses on the difficulties of describing black life in *The Bluest Eye*, in *Sula* she focuses on the difficulties of comprehending black life. The tension in *Sula* is embodied in the blank stares of the Medallion citizens: they fail to understand what they see.

The title of the novel is confusing. It implies that Sula is the main character; however, she and her friend Nel are only the center of a number of changing focal points. Focusing exclusively upon Sula has led to numerous critical disagreements. Wilfred Samuels and Clenora Hudson-Weems describe her as an "authentic-heroic personality" (31). On the other hand, critics such as Dorothy Lee, Valerie Smith, and Keith Byerman view her as a character who fails to find selfhood—Lee calls her "poignantly hollow."[2] Philip Royster sees her as a scapegoat figure (133). Karen Stein finds in Sula epic qualities (148). There is more than a degree of truth in many of these positions. However, in general they fail to place Sula thoroughly into the context that the novel provides for her. The novel does not force readers to judge Sula as either good or bad; rather, it invites them to see her as a part of a very complex social structure. Sula is not the center of the picture; she is only one part of it.

Morrison's narrator spends what may seem an inordinate amount of space describing the families of both Nel and Sula so that characters such as Eva, Sula's grandmother, and Helene, Nel's mother, become almost as familiar as Nel and Sula. Such an emphasis might be expected in a long novel, but in a novel of less than one hundred and seventy pages it is unexpected. Even more unusual are other aspects of the novel. The character Shadrack, who bears no direct relation to Nel or Sula, is the focus of the entire second chapter. His antics, which seemingly have no important bearing on Nel and Sula's friendship, are recounted sporadically in the rest of the novel; and he appears in the last pages. The community is at center stage in the first chapter and remains relevant throughout the novel, particularly in the last chapter. And finally, the novel is structured according to an odd array of years. We begin with a chapter on the community. It bears no heading—presumably it is a prologue. Then we move to a chapter entitled 1919, then to chapters entitled 1920, 1921, and 1923. Part Two begins with a chapter entitled 1937 and moves to 1938, 1939, 1940, and 1941. Then we jump to 1965, the last chapter. Morrison embeds her narrative of Nel and Sula in a context that compels us to evaluate Sula within the context of time and community. Since the community is the outgrowth of a "nigger joke," since white visitors fail to understand what they see there, since the very title of the novel directs attention to Sula and not the community, there is a constant tendency on the part of the reader to underestimate the community's importance. The tension in *The Bluest Eye* grows out of the contrast between the primer version of reality and the reality of black life. In *Sula*, white culture receives scant attention. Its impact on the Bottom and the people who live there is clear, but the citizens of the Bottom are the focus in the novel.

We literally begin the novel with Shadrack and the community. Both reveal the distorting effects of the white world. The patterns of inversion that Jacqueline De Weaver discusses in her article "The Inverted World of Toni Morrison's *The Bluest Eye* and *Sula*" are clearly evident in the way the community receives its name (402). The narrator's attitude toward this detail of the narrative is curious. She calls it "A joke. A nigger joke" (4). But later in chapter one, she paraphrases the thoughts of the white hunters who visit the Bottom: "Maybe it was the bottom of heaven" (6). It is this ambiguous tone, somewhere between derision and seriousness, that prepares us for Shadrack. His response to the white world moves beyond ambiguity to parody.

Shadrack too is a victim of the white world. A soldier in World War One, he risks his life for his country. When he returns, damaged by shell shock, he is hospitalized and placed in a straitjacket. When the hospital becomes overcrowded, the staff gives him $217 and dismisses him. He is promptly arrested and sent back to the Bottom. He has risked his life for a country in which he is quite literally abandoned, left to nurse his war memories in the nether world of the Bottom. Shadrack's great contribution to the Bottom is the invention of National Suicide Day. The naming of the Bottom is an inversion of reality by a white landowner; he says that hill land is bottom land and bequeaths it to his slave. National Suicide Day is a black inversion of white reality. It parodies white holidays such as the Fourth of July and Memorial Day. Those days are celebrations of freedom. The noose Shadrack carries with him calls into question the whole idea of freedom, for it is the tool of the lynch mob as well as of the law. Significantly, Shadrack's celebration is integrated carefully into Bottom life and traditions, much in the same way that the name of the community is accepted despite its inaccuracy. The people of the Bottom absorbed National Suicide Day "into their thoughts, into their language, into their lives" (15).

The real significance of Shadrack's National Suicide Day cannot be grasped until we place it in the context of Sula's life. Just as National Suicide Day becomes a part of community conversation and folklore, so the community labels Sula as a pariah and thereby makes her a part of town lore. Morrison's narrator describes the labelling as a process. Sula's sleeping with Jude causes the town to call Sula "a roach." The men then "fingerprint her for all time" when they learn that she sleeps also with white men (112). Throughout this process a mythic element is at work. Townspeople remember that when Sula returned to town, robins died in large numbers. They begin to lay broomsticks across their doorways at night to keep her away. Other rumors develop: that she had no childhood diseases, that gnats and mosquitoes avoid her. Then finally, she is linked to Shadrack. Dessie sees Sula and Shadrack pass on the street. Instead of insulting Sula as he does most people, Shadrack tips an imaginary hat at her. The conclusion of the neighborhood gossips is that these are "two devils" (117).

Both Sula and Shadrack have community roles. According to the narrator, the town's perception of Sula's evil "changed them in accountable yet mysterious ways" (117). Surprisingly, it improves them morally: "They began to cherish their husbands and wives, protect their children, repair their homes and in general band together against the devil in their midst" (117-118). Such a reaction is more than merely a positive response to Sula's negative example. It reflects an orientation toward reality that contains a rationale for Shadrack, Sula, and the distortion inflicted by the white world. Though Shadrack and Sula are labelled as diabolical, there is no attempt to run them out of town or to purge the community of their influence. Rather, they are accepted as a necessary part of the social structure: "As always the black people looked at evil stony-eyed and let it run" (113). Indeed, Sula's role is connected to that of God: "They would no more run Sula out of town than they would kill the robins that brought her back, for in their secret awareness of Him, He was not the God of three faces they sang about. They knew quite well that He had four, and that the fourth explained Sula" (118). Importantly, the last sentence of this passage suggests that the Bottom is more than a series of responses to the white world. The narrator's ambiguity, Shadrack's celebration of National Suicide Day—both of these are in some respects reactions to the white world. But Sula presents no parody of the white world, nor does she respond with disgust to a world in which she is forced to live on the bottom. She is a force of nature that must be reckoned with, explained by what Morrison calls "the fourth" face of God.[3] Such a dimension of God is

exactly what the Bottom acknowledges. It is represented by Sula
and her habit of doing the unexpected, the unacceptable. But it is
also sanctioned by nature itself, for as the narrator notes "They
[the people in the Bottom] did not believe Nature was ever
askew—only inconvenient. Plague and drought were as 'natural'
as springtime" (90). In *The Bluest Eye* we learn that there are no
stories that do not conform to the order of the primer. Here
Morrison shows us a community where distortion, parody,
rebellion, plague, and drought all have roles. There is a place for
disorder.

Such an understanding of the Bottom sheds light on the
dominant narrative focus of the novel: Sula's friendship with Nel.
As many critics have noted, this friendship is the classic yoking of
opposites, a kind of dialectic in which Nel is the good and socially
correct character and in which Sula is the bad girl who trans-
gresses against the town's morality. If Sula is explained by God's
fourth face, then Nel would be explained by a more traditional
face of God. She is a good citizen, one who works to be a positive
force in the community. But late in the novel Morrison calls into
question Nel's good works. Long after Sula's death, while Nel is
visiting the elderly for her church, she confronts Eva, Sula's
grandmother. Eva is old and senile, but like the old, deranged
prophets of the Bible, her insight is chilling. She confuses Nel with
Sula and accuses Nel of having drowned Chicken Little, the little
boy Sula slung into the river. This statement forces Nel to confront
what she has lived her life denying: that the distinction between
saint and sinner may be nothing more than a definition of terms.
She and Sula shared the same man—Nel the good wife, Sula the
bad girl—and they shared in the same secret crime—the drowning
of Chicken Little. Nel had thought that since she was not swinging
Chicken Little when he fell in the river, the crime was not hers.
Eva reminds Nel that passively watching him sink was as wicked
as letting him go. Sula and Nel are at opposite ends of the social

spectrum in the Bottom. One is a pariah; the other does good deeds. But beneath these definitions, in Eva's eyes, they share the same guilt. Still, the Bottom contains them both.

The larger structure of the community makes this opposition between Nel and Sula significant. In the first two pages of the novel, the narrator presents hypothetical citizens of Medallion reacting to what they see in the Bottom. The Medallion citizens could hear singing and banjos on "quiet days." And if a Medallion citizen ventured up into the Bottom to collect an insurance payment, he might see *things* that he would not understand: "a dark woman in a flowered dress doing a bit of cakewalk, a bit of black bottom, a bit of messing around" to the sound of a mouth harp (4). His failure to understand would be based on his failure to connect opposites: "The black people watching her would laugh and rub their knees, and it would be easy for the valley man to hear the laughter and not notice the adult pain that rested some-where under the eyelids"(4). The social order in the Bottom embraces opposites: laughter and pain, good and evil, Nel and Sula. The order invoked at the beginning of *The Bluest Eye* denies any order contrary to itself. Thus, the insight the valley man might miss is the insight that Morrison centers her whole novel around: "the laughter [that] was part of the pain" (4). This laughter is the basis of the whole culture: "A shucking, knee-slapping, wet-eyed laughter that could even describe and explain how they came to be where they were" (4).

Though Medallion influences the development of personalities in the Bottom, Morrison suggests that there is a resourcefulness here that Medallion does not understand, an ability to accept and survive pain and evil, to accept the unusual that the white world cannot even see. Thus, *Sula* becomes, among other things, a portrait of a failure of insight on the part of the white world. Moreover, this failure of insight has devastating effects, for the first line of the novel tells us how this saga will end: "In that place, where they tore the nightshade and blackberry patches from their roots to make room for the Medallion City Golf Course, there was once a neighborhood" (3). Our vantage point throughout this novel is retrospective. We see the Bottom from the standpoint of its demise. And its demise is a disruption of a natural order, a tearing away of roots, a refusal to accept the diversity of life represented in this opening sentence by nightshade and blackberry. At the end of the novel, the Bottom has "collapsed," and the white people have begun to take over the hills again. The fragmentation of the Bottom is connected to an altered sense of community that Nel notices on her walk to the nursing home to see Eva. The Bottom had been "a real place," she observes. Now it has been left to "the poor, the old, the stubborn—and the rich white folks" who suddenly want houses in the hills. Now there are no more communities: "just separate televisions and separate telephones and less and less dropping by" (166).

In "Unspeakable Things Unspoken: The Afro-American Presence in American Literature," Morrison has spoken of her dissatisfaction with the first chapter of *Sula*. She describes it as a vestibule, a door, an attempt to make the world she presents in this novel understandable to a "mainstream" audience (221-223). Such an observation underscores for us the importance of what Medallion citizens fail to see. Morrison is not just writing about a world whose existence average white readers might not be aware of; she is writing about a world they might not understand. Morrison is reflecting the same two-world orientation we find in *The Bluest Eye*: part of the world is modeled on the primer; the rest of the world is ignored. The white characters in *Sula* cannot understand what they see in the Bottom: it is incomprehensible—like words without spacing, punctuation, and capitalization. The "valley man" in the first chapter who has business up in the hills hears the laughter, but he cannot see the pain. There is an important difference between *Sula* and *The Bluest Eye*. Here Morrison presents a clearly articulated alternative to the world of the primer. It is a world apart, separate, unknown by the white world. But it does exist.

In his study of the Medieval and Renaissance culture out of which Rabelais' work grows, Bakhtin finds a two-world orientation that shares many of the traits of the two worlds in Morrison's novel. Bakhtin's explanation helps us better understand the Bottom. Bakhtin finds in Medieval and Renaissance culture "a second world and a second life outside of officialdom" (*Rabelais* 6). Moreover, this second world is not an artistic creation or rendering: "it does not acknowledge any distinction between actors and spectators" (*Rabelais* 7). In short, it *is* a state of being, not an imitation of a state of being. Finally, it involves in some instances the creation of the very figure which we see in Morrison's novel: the devil. Bakhtin traces the diabolical back to the mystery plays (*Rabelais* 265-266). But he makes the important point that in Medieval and Renaissance culture this diabolical figure ultimately leaves the stage and becomes a part of life: "It crossed the footlights to merge with the life of the marketplace" (*Rabelais* 267). According to Bakhtin, the two traits that allow this figure to become "a popular comic figure" are "his ambivalence and his material bodily element" (*Rabelais* 267). Moreover, he is ultimately transformed into the carnivalesque figure of Harlequin. Harlequin and other popular-festive images allow people "to express their criticism, their deep distrust of official truth" (*Rabelais* 269). In these images freedom is not an "exterior right" but rather "an inner content of the image" (*Rabelais* 269). In *The Dialogic Imagination* (and also at points in *Rabelais and his World*), Bakhtin enlarges the range of popular-festive images that descend to us from Medieval and Renaissance literature. He includes the rogue, the clown, and the fool (*Dialogic* 158). All of these figures are associated with just what we see in the Bottom: "the theatrical trappings of the public square" (*Dialogic* 159).

What is more, to Bakhtin the most distinctive feature of these characters is their expression of "the right to be other" (*Dialogic* 159). In short, like the Bottom itself, the "second" world Bakhtin describes recognizes difference, those figures who do not find themselves mirrored in the world of mainstream society.

There are important connections between what we see in the Bottom and Bakhtin's ideas. Like the fools and rogues Bakhtin describes, Sula and Shadrack are not stage figures: they are interactive products of character and society. Sula is made into a pariah. Shadrack sets out to be the town fool, creating a ritual to display himself, a ritual that becomes a part of the town activities. Moreover, both represent boldly what Bakhtin calls the "material bodily element." Sula ignores all sexual standards of the world around her. Shadrack forces people to focus on death and dying on the third day of each year. Furthermore, in the case of Shadrack's National Suicide Day, we have a ritual that expresses freedom in "the inner content of the image." Just as Bakhtin suggests, this image does not express an "external right" to freedom. In fact, on the final celebration of National Suicide Day when it does indeed become a protest march and moves into the white part of town, Shadrack quickly recognizes that something is wrong: he stands and watches the people he has inspired, "Having forgotten his song and rope" (162). Most of the celebrants are killed as they attempt to destroy the bridge built at the New River Road, an emblem of their exclusion from the white world. They had wanted to work on the bridge while it was being built; ironically, the place becomes the site of their death as well as the end of National Suicide Day. As soon as National Suicide Day becomes an expression of what Bakhtin calls "an external right" to freedom, it vanishes.

Perhaps more important than either Shadrack or Sula is the Bottom itself. It is that "second world" that Bakhtin discusses, a world that contains diversity: Nel and Sula, blackberry and nightshade. It exists outside of officialdom, not as the creation of an artist as satire or parody but as lives lived in the public square, lives transformed through folk idiom into mythic creations that correspond to Harlequin, to the fool, or the rogue, lives that embody what Bakhtin calls "the right to be other" (*Dialogic* 159). We see the public square in the first scene in the novel where the very people on the street are turning pain to laughter through their public dancing, singing, and harmonica playing. This world is quite different from the one we see at the end of the novel where "there weren't any places left, just separate houses with separate televisions and less and less dropping by" (166). Thus, the ambiguity of the narrator's tone in the opening chapter is extremely important: perhaps there is a double irony in the white man's "nigger joke." Maybe the world of the Bottom is indeed the "bottom of heaven." Perhaps the communal spirit that resides there is something the white world has never known and consequently cannot recognize.

Still, the irony does not end with the joke. In *Figures in Black*, Henry Louis Gates ties the very figure of Harlequin to the black tradition. According to Gates, many scholars believe that Harlequin was originally a black slave. Moreover, he came to be associated with those attributes which Renaissance painters associated with blacks: the satyr and the cat. Gates shows that Harlequin ultimately became a trope: "So stylized did Harlequin's role become that he could simply point to one of the black patches on his suit and become invisible" (51). In short, Harlequin ceased to be anything more than a stock representation of blacks. When this figure moves into American culture, Harlequin is debased. Gates says that the figure moves from "archetype to stereotype" (52). No longer is he the noble clown. Instead, he is the black minstrel, in short a "nigger joke." There are no minstrels in Morrison's novel. But Gates' discussion of Harlequin informs us of a central irony in the novel. The white citizens who view the Bottom fail to understand what they see there. To them it is a "nigger joke," as invisible as Harlequin is when he points to the patches on his suit. But ironically, the joke is on the white visitors: they fail to understand the meaning or the origin of the laughter.

The final tragedy of the novel thus becomes the disappearance of the Bottom. Furthermore, at this point the issue of time becomes important. In his essay "Forms of Time and Chronotope in the Novel" Bakhtin connects modes of production to both time and ritual (*Dialogic* 206-214). In a culture that is primarily agricultural, "time is *profoundly spatial and concrete. It is not separated from the earth or from nature*" (*Dialogic* 208). Moreover, man's life itself—his very perception—becomes a communal entity, a part of "the collective process of labor and the battle against nature" (*Dialogic* 208). As man moves away from nature, this matrix begins to break apart. The natural world is a backdrop for human life rather than an integral part of it. Time is connected to the cycles of nature only through ritual. The final end of this whole process in Bakhtin's eyes is the individual human life:

> As class society develops further and as ideological spheres are increasingly differentiated, the internal disintegration (bifurcation) of each element of the matrix becomes more and more intense: food and drink, the sexual act in their real aspect enter personal everyday life, they become predominantly a *personal* and *everyday* affair, they acquire a specific narrowly quotidian coloration, they become the petty humdrum "coarse" realities of life. (*Dialogic* 213)

In short, communal reality is replaced by individual perception and experience. The public square is presented in this novel as a communal reality that white visitors have no ability to understand. Indeed for them to understand such a world, they must participate: "stand in the back of Greater Saint Matthew's and let the tenor's voice dress him [the visitor] in silk, or touch the hands of the spoon carvers (who had not worked in eight years) and let the fingers that danced on wood kiss his skin" (4). According to

Morrison's narrator, only through such experiences could those visitors begin to understand "the laughter [that] was part of the pain" (4). Communal reality is what is lost in the disappearance of the Bottom.

We see only part of the demise of the Bottom in *Sula*. We never see the Bottom as an agricultural entity, for it is from the first an agricultural joke: no one can grow crops in the hills. This is why the land is given to the dispossessed blacks who live there. However, this community was originally a part of a farm, an agricultural enterprise. Moreover, the Bottom as it is presented is also a communal unit. The rituals surrounding Sula's sex life and Shadrack's madness make these more than isolated events. Also, Sula's return to the Bottom after a ten-year absence is heralded by an aberration in the natural world, a "plague of robins" (89). Her death is foreshadowed by an early snow that has devastating effects upon the community. The narrator is quick to comment on the connection the community perceives between nature and human life: "although they were accustomed to excesses in nature...they still dreaded the way a relatively trivial phenomenon could become sovereign in their lives and bend their minds to its will" (89). Nel also connects changes in nature to Sula's return; she sees "a sheen, a glimmering" (94), "a magic" (95) that she "did not wonder at" (95). She "knows" it is due to Sula's return. This change in nature occurs at the beginning of Part Two, the portion of the novel that describes the demise of the Bottom.

Finally, the end of the Bottom is ultimately tied to a shift in modes of production. Bottom men are distinguished from valley men by their jobs. The whites in town will not hire Jude and the other Bottom men to work on the New River Road. Jude must work as a waiter, a job he considers to be menial. The lack of work causes BoyBoy, Eva's husband, to leave Eva with three children to feed. And the spoon carvers at the beginning of the novel have not worked in eight years. Thus, there is that shared status of all in the Bottom. They are all victims of "a nigger joke," a joke that is associated by the narrator with unemployment and failed crops: "Just a nigger joke. The kind white folks tell when the mill closes down and they're looking for a little comfort somewhere. The kind colored folks tell on themselves when the rain doesn't come, or comes for weeks, and they're looking for a little comfort somehow" (4-5). Shadrack's yearly ritual can be looked at as an expression of this joke. With each new year he reminds the people of the Bottom of their oppression.

Curiously, what Morrison's narrator calls the "collapse" of the Bottom coincides with their integration into the fabric of Medallion. The chapter entitled 1965 begins with these lines:

> Things were so much better in 1965. Or so it seemed. You could go downtown and see colored people working in the dime store behind the counter, even handling money with cash-register keys around their necks. And a colored man taught mathematics at the junior high school. (163)

Once again the narrator's ambiguity is important. Things "seem" better because work is better. But what has vanished is that communal spirit that characterized the joke-victimized citizens of the Bottom. We see many of the old characters in 1965, but they fail to recognize one another as they would have in the time of the Bottom. Shadrack passes Nel, but he cannot remember who she is. As they move in "opposite directions," both are thinking "separate thoughts." The distance between them "increases" (174). Nel remembers Sula. She even thinks that Sula makes the trees move; once again the narrator implies that there is a connection between human life and nature. But Nel's crying at the end of the novel seems to grow out of an individual grief that lacks any kind of communal structure: "it had no bottom and it had no top" (174). Furthermore, it leads her to no conclusion, no catharsis: it is "just circles and circles of sorrow" (174).

In "Forms of Time and Chronotope in the Novel" Bakhtin traces through ritual and myth the matrices of time and space. He argues that in the modern novel we get glimpses of the communal structures that once tied us to nature. Morrison's novel gives us one of these glimpses. She begins with the "nigger joke" of the Bottom and shows us the cultural fabric that develops in its midst before the community and its rituals vanish as lives become individualized and people sit alone before separate televisions. But her novel is more than just a portrait of a culture. It is the portrait of a failed insight. For ultimately to understand the "nigger joke" in this novel, we must do more than hear the laughter that the hypothetical valley man hears. We must perceive the pain that gives birth to it and the wholeness of the culture in which it resides. Then we know what was lost in the demise of the Bottom.

In her recently published essay *Playing in the Dark*, Morrison argues that "Black Slavery enriched the country's creative possibilities. For in that construction of blackness *and* enslavement could be found not only the not-free but also, with the dramatic polarity created by skin color, the projection of the not-me" (38). In short, African-Americans and their culture represented all of those things that white Americans did not want to recognize about their culture: that freedom was bought with enslavement, that prosperity was bought with poverty, that life for some was bought with death for others—in short, that white was defined by what it was not: black. The top indeed rests upon the "Bottom," but only for so long as it cannot see the world of the Bottom as anything more than a joke. Morrison suggests in *Sula* the cost of such blindness. To build the Medallion City Golf Course, "they tore the nightshade and blackberry patches from their roots" (4). One of these plants is poisonous and the other bears nutritious fruit (Morrison, "Unspeakable" 221). In order to play golf in peace, the city fathers sacrificed both the poison and the fruit; in failing to recognize the pain, they lost the ability to understand the laughter.

Morrison's novel shows us both: the pain and the laughter, the nightshade and the blackberry, Sula and Nel. Thus, understanding the Bottom forces the reader to understand the ideological blindness of "the masters."

The Bluest Eye is a novel in which individual lives are shattered. Claudia attempts to put them back together, but ultimately she fails, for the only story she knows is that of the primer. The tension in the novel grows out of the contrast between the primer version of reality and the reality presented in the novel. *Sula* is also a novel about shattered lives. Sula dies an early death. Nel lives on, but it is a life that lacks fullness. The only love she has left is that which she feels for her children: "like a pan of syrup kept too long on the stove" (165). The Bottom vanishes. But while it exists, the Bottom is, in the narrator's words, "a real place" (166). Much like the characters in *The Bluest Eye*, the characters in the Bottom must improvise their lives, imposing a kind of order by using whatever is at hand. Shadrack creates National Suicide Day. Eva sacrifices a leg to raise a family. She burns one child up and jumps out a window to save another from burning. As narrator of *The Bluest Eye*, Claudia tells us that her story does not work, but such is not the case with the narrator of *Sula*. She tells us that visitors did not understand, that visitors forgot, that a golf course covered what was, but that "there was once a neighborhood" (3). Thus, the pattern of tension we saw in *The Bluest Eye* is reversed. There, black experience was shown to be unintelligible in the context of white reality. Here, the reverse is true. Black experience becomes the focus, and white misunderstanding the point. The embodiment of white culture in *The Bluest Eye* is the passage from the primer. In this novel it is the uncomprehending stares of those valley men who visit the Bottom.

Morrison is aware that the Bottom is a world that is hard to understand, so she provides her "mainstream" readers with what she calls a "door" ("Unspeakable" 221-223). Like the white visitors from Medallion, such readers look at a world they have not seen before. But if they stay long enough to become involved, if they touch the hands of the spoon carvers, then what they see is their own failed insight.

Notes

1. Numerous critics have argued that the novel itself resists
interpretive strategies. Barbara McDowell argues that it works
against the dominant critical paradigm in African-American
literature. According to her, within *Sula* there are no neat divisions
between black and white, and literature ceases to be the vehicle of
racial unity and liberty. Emphasizing paradox and ambiguity, the
novel presents to us a world where we never get to the "bottom"
of things (151). Robert Grant writes that *Sula* is "sui generis"
because it refuses to be "amenable to some ideological translation"
(93).

2. I refer here to these articles and books:

Keith E. Byerman, "Beyond Realism: The Fiction of Toni
Morrison," *Toni Morrison*, ed. Harold Bloom (New York: Chelsea,
1990);

Dorothy H. Lee, "The Quest for Self: Triumph and Failure in
the Works of Toni Morrison," *Black Women Writers (1950-1980):
A Critical Evaluation*, ed. Mari Evans (New York: Doubleday,
1984);

Valerie Smith, *Self-Discovery and Authority in Afro-American
Narrative* (Cambridge: Harvard, 1987).

3. Morrison has said to Claudia Tate that characters such as
Sula, Cholly Breedlove, Guitar Bains, and Ajax all have about
them "'a nice wildness…. It's pre-Christ in the best sense. It's
Eve'" (qtd in Otten 37).

FOUR

Song of Solomon:

Making Connections

In a 1978 interview with Jane Bakerman, Morrison said that *Song of Solomon* differs from her previous novels: "I made a serious attempt to write it all out and not to write in a hermetic, closed way" (58). She implies here that her first two novels were unapproachable in some respects and that *Song of Solomon* is not. The first two chapters of this study have focused on the ways in which *The Bluest Eye* and *Sula* defy reader expectation: Claudia's failure to find the correct form for the story of Pecola; the contradictory, ambiguous world of the Bottom. But in what ways is *Song of Solomon* different from these novels? In what ways is it open to readers as Morrison implies? The central difference is its adherence to traditional methods of plot and character development.

Many critics have noted the traditional characteristics of *Song of Solomon*. Marilyn Mobley argues that Milkman's life conforms to the mythic pattern that Joseph Campbell identifies in *The Hero with a Thousand Faces*. He leaves home, is initiated, and returns (77, 142).[1] The presence of a traditional hero in this novel distinguishes it from the first two. Both Barbara Rigney and Linda Wagner identify this novel as a *Bildungsroman*, the story of a young man who leaves home to seek education and fortune in the city (Rigney 34, Wagner 200). Milkman does not go to the city;

he leaves it. Nonetheless, in the fashion of the protagonist of the *Bildungsroman*, he does seek his fortune in a world separate from that in which he is raised. Peter Bruck calls *Song of Solomon* a novel of initiation, a coming of age novel (294). This is another traditional quality of this work. The hero moves from a youth of misdirection to a moment of decision and a sense of direction. Gary Brenner finds in *Song of Solomon* an underlying pattern common to the stories of Oedipus, Perseus, Tristan, Romulus, and others: the saga of the birth and development of the hero, the pattern Otto Rank calls the "monomyth" (115). Milkman's birth and development are at the center of the novel. The narrator begins the story on the day of his birth and ends it on what may very well be the day of his death. The earlier novels (and the later ones) are not so clearly focused on one character or one situation. Though many of these critics acknowledge that Morrison's use of these traditional patterns is far from traditional, the choices she has made are worth our notice. This novel is consciously traditional in a way the earlier novels are not. Why?

In some respects, *Song of Solomon* complements *The Bluest Eye* and *Sula*. In those novels black life was shown to be incompatible with white expectations, with white forms of expression. But in *Song of Solomon* Morrison uses traditional forms so that she may show their incompleteness, their incompatibility with black life, in particular the lives of black women. Morrison has said that she chose a man to make the journey in *Song of Solomon* because "'he had more to learn than a woman would have'" (Rigney 36). In similar fashion she chose traditional forms because her story would emphasize their incompleteness. Moreover, Morrison chooses to explore landscapes and themes very familiar to readers of American literature for the same reason: she wants to show their incompleteness.

Even a cursory glance at the novel demonstrates its links with mainstream American literature. Norman Harris has pointed out that Milkman is ultimately outside of black cultural traditions in the first half of the novel. His parents have placed him in a world of materialism and privilege that contrasts sharply with the folk, agrarian culture that he discovers in Danville and Shalimar in the last half of the novel (8-9). Thus, his journey takes him back to his roots, a familiar pattern in twentieth-century American literature: the alien, the outsider seeking a home in a past that he has lost touch with. The narrator of Jean Toomer's *Cane* makes a journey very similar to Milkman's: he discovers his roots in rural Georgia. In fact, *Cane* grows out of Toomer's own attempt to understand his past. A young boy who never knew his father, who was raised in the rapidly vanishing splendor of his grandfather's urban Washington, D. C., Toomer found a special resonance in Georgia because it was the land his father had come from, because it was a land where the remnants of the slave age were still palpable in the air. Thus, as he describes the landscape of rural Georgia in Parts One and Three of *Cane*, the shadowy narrator of *Cane* is very much like Milkman in Danville or Shalimar. He is discovering a past he never knew he had. He is quite literally putting himself together again.

David Cowart has tied Milkman's discovery of folk songs in Shalimar to Ike McCaslin's analysis of farm ledgers in Faulkner's *Go Down, Moses!* (91). And indeed the two discoveries have much in common, for both characters discover that understanding the self involves understanding the past. Milkman can only understand the song of Solomon after he has visited the land where Solomon lived, after he has learned the place names that reflect the actions of his ancestors. Similarly, Ike McCaslin must read the ledgers of his ancestors to understand their relationship to the land and its inhabitants. This understanding enables him to grasp the meaning the land should have for him.

Milkman's search for his roots ultimately leads us to landscapes that are very familiar in much American fiction. Lincoln's

Heaven is, in Milkman's father's description of it, a veritable
paradise: "'We had a pond that was four acres. And a stream full
of fish. Right down in the heart of the valley. Prettiest mountain
you ever saw.... And all around in the mountains was deer and
turkey.... And we had fruit trees'"(51). Depictions of the American landscape as paradise are widespread. The very first descriptions of it suggest this image. In his "Narrative of the 1584
Voyage" Arthur Barlowe describes the American landscape in this
fashion: "The earth bringeth foorth all things in aboundance, as in
the first creation, without toile or labour"(8). But there is more
than an image of America as paradise in Milkman's grandfather's
farm. Lincoln's Heaven is a place where Macon and Pilate and
their father are self-supporting and independent. Macon tells
Milkman, "I worked right alongside my father" (51). Later he
describes food the farm produced: wild turkey ("the meat...was
tender, sweet, and juicy" [51]), "the best pork outside of Virginia"
(52), and even cherry pie (Pilate made one using fruit from their
trees). Still later in the novel when Milkman visits Danville, the
townspeople have granted to Milkman's grandfather almost
legendary significance: "Macon Dead was the farmer they wanted
to be, the clever irrigator, the peachtree grower, the wild-turkey
roaster" (235). Moreover, his farm has come to symbolize
independence, self-sufficiency, success: "'You see?' the farm said
to them. 'See? See what you can do? Never mind you can't tell
one letter from another, never mind you born a slave,.... Here,
this here, is what a man can do if he puts his mind to it and his
back in it'" (235). The land itself has meaning because it represents human endeavor. From quite early, American writers have
viewed the land in this way. In *Notes on the State of Virginia*,
Thomas Jefferson says that "Those who labor the earth are the
chosen people of God,..., whose breasts He has made his peculiar
deposit for substantial and genuine virtue" (743). Jefferson even
suggests that Americans should leave manufacturing to Europe

because of the abundance of land in America and the way in which land bestows virtue upon those who cultivate it. Jefferson's idea is repeated by later writers. Thoreau argues in the "Economy" chapter of *Walden* that a person may support himself quite well with nine rows of beans and a little hard work. Thomas Sutpen in Faulkner's *Absolom, Absolom!* is similar to Milkman's grandfather: he comes seemingly from nowhere, takes a parcel of land and develops it. Land acquires value over generations because it represents this unremitting effort to support oneself, to survive, ultimately to prosper: the ledgers that Ike McCaslin examines in some respects represent this same effort. Thus, the landscape is a kind of paradise; its memory brings a rare smile to Milkman's father's face. But it is more than that. It is a symbol of self-sufficiency.

Leo Marx argues in *The Machine in the Garden* that pastoral self-sufficiency is only one part of the national consciousness. The other half is industry, development, and eventual greed—the destruction of the garden. Lincoln's Heaven also reminds us of these forces. It is the greed of others that kills Macon's father—greed for his land, his paradise. Other people—the Butlers—want to develop the land. The house that Circe inhabits is the product of their greed, and she is purposely presiding over its demise. And it is greed that Milkman's father learns and embodies, the same greed that killed his own father. He develops rental property by shrewd buying and ruthless collection of rent. Early in the novel we see him threatening to evict Guitar's family from their home. By the end of the conversation in which he describes Lincoln's Heaven to Milkman, he is supplying the other half of the puzzle: "Own things. And let the things you own own other things" (55). This is the machine that is inevitably a part of the garden: Milkman's father is devouring his community for his own profit. Thus, there is ambivalence in Macon's character. He remembers the beauty of Lincoln's Heaven, but he also practices the ethic of those men who destroyed it. Milkman is the victim of this same contradiction. Though he discovers his past, his roots in the agrarian and the rural, the initial motivation for his journey is in large part greed, the very force that killed his grandfather. In fact, just after Milkman discovers in Danville that his grandfather was a legendary farmer, he tells about his own father, making him also into a legend: "Milkman found himself rattling off assets like an accountant, describing deals, total rents income" (236). And then moments later, Milkman's greed asserts itself: "Milkman wanted the gold. He wanted to get up right then and there and go get it" (236). Thus, Milkman, like his father before him, contains within himself a duality that is very American. He sees the beauty of Lincoln's Heaven; he relishes the tales of his legendary grandfather and the farm he built. Nonetheless, he wants the gold he thinks it contains. He values the past and the land, but most of all he values money. This duality is one primary source of tension in the novel.

Milkman's initiation into the rural world also ties the novel to a number of traditions. When Milkman comes to Danville and Shalimar, the communities he sees are made up of black people. In Shalimar, he swaps insults with the men of the town and eventually winds up fighting them with a coke bottle. Thus, he proves himself worthy of inclusion in the hunt. The swapping of insults is a traditional test of manhood in Shalimar. This ritual is tied to "sounding," "signifying," and "the dozens," all traditional methods of taunting, boasting, and insulting within the black community (Bell 22). To solve the riddle of his past, Milkman must memorize and interpret a song that is presented to him by children in call and response fashion. Once again, Morrison is drawing on traditions within the black community: call and response singing dates back to slave culture.

Milkman's participation in the hunt ties the work to other traditions. *Sir Gawain and the Green Knight* presents a kind of allegory which examines the self in the figure of the animal hunted. In similar fashion, Milkman confronts himself on the hunt. Stripped of his city clothes and his watch, hunted by Guitar, he discovers as he hears the dogs bay that "all a man had was what he was born with" (277). The cleaning of the bobcat becomes an examination of the self. For every portion of the animal that is cut away, Milkman remembers one of Guitar's statements. Each of these statements forces Milkman to confront himself honestly without the weight of his past, to question himself: "*What good is a man's life if he can't choose what to die for?*'" (283). At the end of this scene Milkman remembers the peacock he and Guitar saw on the hood of a Buick. Morrison uses this image to remind the reader of Guitar's statement about the bird: "'Can't nobody fly with all that shit [the tail of the bird]. Wanna fly, you got to give up all the shit that weighs you down'" (179). The "shit" that weighs Milkman down is his past, that world of materialism, greed, and class that his parents have surrounded him with. It is also his vanity, a trait that Morrison implies is common in males, for Guitar points out that only the male peacock has the tail feathers that weigh him down. Milkman begins to shed his immediate past and his vanity in Shalimar, even as he finds his ancestral past. On the hunting trip he is forced quite literally to leave his city clothes behind. He wears borrowed clothes: World War II army fatigues, brogans, and a knit cap. What is more, like the bobcat, Milkman is now being hunted, for Guitar wants his life. He truly knows how it feels to have only what one is born with.

Milkman's experience on the hunt is reminiscent of Faulkner's *Go Down, Moses!*. When Ike McCaslin seeks Old Ben, he is forced to leave behind first his gun, then later his compass and watch. These are the trappings of civilization and much like Milkman's city clothes, they separate Ike from the wilderness. Only when he has left them behind can he encounter Old Ben, an experience that transforms him. In similar fashion only after Milkman has separated himself from his city ways and his city clothes can he truly understand his past. Ironically, only when he is quite literally in the position of a hunted animal can he do what Guitar has challenged him to do with his life: "'Live it!'" (183).

Morrison has thus located her novel in very traditional territory. She has drawn a portrait of a young man discovering his roots in an agrarian setting where land represents human endeavor. Her young man is in some respects like the narrator of *Walden* and like Ike McCaslin from *Go Down, Moses!* in that he is seeking to understand himself, to lose the accumulated weight of vanity and custom. But again, we return to the question we began with: why does Morrison make these choices? The answer lies in the language of the novel.

In the first chapter of *Song of Solomon*, Morrison sets forth a pattern of negation that reappears throughout the novel. Though many critics have noticed this pattern, none has fully tied it to the structure of the novel.[2] In actuality it is a verbal expression of the oppressive force of white society, much like the passage from the primer that appears at the beginning of *The Bluest Eye* or the white citizens of Medallion who appear in the first chapter of *Sula*. Doctor Street is named by the people who live in its vicinity because the only black doctor in town resides there. Language works naturally here, for place names reflect the lives of inhabitants. But the white city fathers object, insisting that it be called Mains Avenue and not Doctor Street. The people of the neighborhood thus come to call it Not Doctor Street. The "charity hospital" is called by neighborhood people "No Mercy Hospital" because it refuses to admit blacks. In both of these cases language is subverted in a rather complex play with words.

Changing Doctor Street to Mains Avenue is a subversion of the natural function of language, for Mains Avenue is an arbitrary name: it has no connection to the people who live there. But the usage "Not Doctor Street" subverts the subversion. Doctor Street is once again named by those who live in its vicinity. The name "No Mercy Hospital" works the same way. It exposes the charity hospital for what it is: a hospital without mercy. Moreover, it grants to the hospital a name composed by the community surrounding the hospital. Bakhtin states in his essay "Discourse in the Novel" that "there are no 'neutral' words and forms." According to him "language...lies on the borderline between oneself and the other. The word in language is half someone else's. It becomes 'one's own' only when the speaker populates it with his own intention, his own accent, when he appropriates the word..." (*Dialogic* 293).[3] Thus, by showing us the double subversion of these names, Morrison is presenting to us the very process that Bakhtin describes. And once again just as the primer version of reality becomes the prism through which we try to view black culture, so here the distortion of language is something we must look through to see the lives in this novel clearly. Again we have tension. There is the reality of the white explanation of the world: Mains Avenue, charity hospital. Both of these are subversions. And then we have the black reclaiming of these names. The words of the master have suddenly been "appropriated." Not Doctor Street is really Doctor Street and charity hospital is really No Mercy hospital. This struggle over words mirrors a larger struggle in the novel: the struggle over theme, landscape, the traditional patterns outlined in the first part of this chapter.

In several passages we see this struggle over language re-enacted. In some cases language is re-appropriated. Macon's father's farm is called Lincoln's Heaven; the family has a horse called President Lincoln, a cow called General Grant, and a pig called General Lee. Macon's father's explanation of the horse's name demonstrates a reclaiming of words: "'Papa said President Lincoln was a good plow hand before he was President and you shouldn't take a good plow hand away from his work'" (51). In other passages the subversion is not merely a matter of language. Pilate is able to get Milkman and Guitar out of jail by playing a part that the white world brought into being: the cooperative black servant. With trembling hands, Pilate verifies the lie that Milkman and Guitar have told the police. The bones they stole were her husband's. She even uses language that the white policemen would expect her to: she could not bury her husband because the "'funeral peoples' wanted fifty dollars" (207). Milkman is astonished by her transformation ("Pilate *had* been shorter"), by her quoting of the Bible (207). Pilate's act is similar to the language we examined earlier: it subverts the subversion. It takes the white stereotyping (that old black women are docile and slow of wit) and uses it to reclaim her nephew and his friend. She fools the police and gets Milkman and Guitar out of jail. Brenda Marshall has shown that Pilate is even able to retain her dignity in this episode by misquoting the Bible in such a way that she sends a veiled message to Milkman, Guitar, and the policeman (486). She attributes to Matthew 21:2 this passage: "'what so e'er the Lord hath put together, let no man put asunder'" (207). Actually, the passage contains Christ's words to two of his disciples: "Go into the village over against you, and straightway ye shall find an ass tied, and a colt with her: *loose* them, and bring *them* unto me" (King James version). Pilate's choice of passages is significant, for it subverts her position as servant by making her the master of language. According to Marshall, she is able to call Milkman and Guitar an ass and a colt without their knowing it.

But *Song of Solomon* also explores other dimensions of the subversion of language. Bakhtin says that the word does not become one's own until "the speaker...appropriates the word" (*Dialogic* 293). Thus, the failure to seize the word and make it one's own results in enslavement to someone else's language. The name the Dead family carries with it exemplifies this failure. Macon is very aware of the haphazard way in which the family got its name through "a literal slip of the pen" (18). A drunken Union soldier transcribed the name incorrectly. Yet the family "had agreed to abide by a naming done to them by somebody who couldn't have cared less" (18). This is quite literally the acceptance of another's word. As the name is passed from generation to generation, the paper and the word on it become objects that enslave the family to the "Dead" name, a name they did not choose. As Circe says, "'White people name Negroes like race horses'" (243). The very process of choosing names in the family is similar. The Bible is opened and a name is randomly chosen. Macon's father uses this process despite the fact that he cannot read a word of the Bible. It is a book that is handed to him by white people, just like the piece of paper from the union soldier. Thus, Macon Dead, like his father before him, is enslaved to words imposed upon him by white people, much as Pecola is enslaved to the primer version of reality: without blue eyes she cannot live. In predictable fashion, Macon, like Pecola, is never able to see beyond the world bequeathed to him by whites. At the end of the novel he is essentially uninterested in the family history that Milkman has discovered. He is far too busy living out the American dream of owning things, the very dream that caused white people to shoot his father. His very office becomes an emblem of his enslavement: he paints "Office" on the door, but it is never called anything but "Sonny's Shop." No one can remember Sonny or his shop. But that legend on the plate glass window is more powerful than anything Macon can provide in its place: "Scraping the previous owner's name off was hardly worth the trouble since he couldn't scrape it from anybody's mind" (17). In these words Morrison describes the process which Bakhtin explains: enslavement to another's words.

Within such a context, Milkman's act of rediscovering the origins of the family names is seemingly liberating and heroic. He finds out the real names of his grandfather and his grandmother, and he enables Pilate to bury the piece of paper her father gave to her, a symbol of misappropriation. Pilate's faith in her nephew is justified, for he does what none of the men before him have done: take the words back, give them their true meaning. Thus, Sing becomes the name of Pilate's mother, not a command from her father. Solomon is identified as the man who flew away, the man for whom Solomon's Leap was named. And Ryna's cries of grief are identified with the wind in Ryna's Gulch. Quite literally the landscape finally reflects the names of those who lived there, Pilate's ancestors. Language works naturally as it did in the original naming of Doctor Street. It connects people to one another and to places. It would seem that Morrison's use of traditional patterns of development, of traditional landscapes, is appropriate, for Milkman does find his roots in the agrarian world of his grandfather. But it is easy to assume too much. Morrison uses various traditions in this novel so that she may show their incompleteness, not so that she can make her characters, her plot, or her theme fit into prefabricated structures.

It is very easy to overestimate Milkman's heroism, to misunderstand what he has learned. Though he is placed in the position of the traditional hero, the young man who discovers himself, finds his roots, in many respects what he discovers is not himself but those around him. Thus, reading the novel properly forces us to come to terms with Milkman's failings as well as his successes. Many of them can be examined through looking at the act Milkman longs for and eventually enacts in the novel: flying.

At first glance, flying seems a part of Milkman's heroism. The novel begins with Mr. Smith's suicidal flight from the top of Mercy Hospital. It ends as Milkman flies into the arms of Guitar, a flight comparable to that of his great-grandfather. This is the pattern of the hero coming of age. He learns to do what his ancestors have done. But flight is an ambiguous symbol in this novel. Morrison alludes to a number of myths and stories in her use of flight. First, she alludes to the many and varied stories of slaves flying back to Africa. Joyce Wegs points out two versions of the story in her article "Toni Morrison's *Song of Solomon*: A Blues Song." In one a male slave flies away after being abused by a white overseer. In another an older black male teaches his community to remember its power of flight (218). There is an important difference between these two stories. In the first, flying provides escape for one man; in the second, the whole community flies away. Michael Awkward argues that Morrison consciously alters the tradition of the flying African story in this novel. The version he calls "traditional" involves a witchdoctor who leads a "mass exodus" from a plantation ("Unruly and Let Loose" 483-484). Placed in the context of this version of the story, Milkman's flight becomes an act of self-expression but not an act of community liberation.

Grace Ann Hovet and Barbara Lounsberry tie flying to the entirety of the African-American tradition (119-121). According to them, though flight in African-American songs and stories is often a metaphor for freedom, it can also be a symbol of self-aggrandizement and escape. For instance, in Richard Wright's *Native Son*, Bigger Thomas speaks of flying as something he could do but for the white world: "'I *could* fly a plane if I had a chance." His friend Gus then enumerates the obstacles that stand between Bigger and an airplane: "If you wasn't black and if you had some money and if they'd let you go to aviation school, you *could* fly a plane" (20). To Bigger, flight is a symbol of freedom; it is a door into the sky, into the world of privilege and opportunity reserved only for whites. Ralph Ellison's character Todd in "Flying Home" succeeds in doing what Bigger cannot do. He is a pilot. But he discovers that his very desire to fly grows out of his need to fly away from the reality of being black in America, leaving behind all that he should be responsible for. Flying to him is an escape. These examples underscore the basic ambiguity in this image: flight can liberate the individual, or it can liberate the community.

Flight in this novel also reminds us of Icarus. Cynthia Davis, Trudier Harris, and Bessie Jones and Audrey Vincent have tied this novel to the Icarus myth. Morrison herself has mentioned that myth in relation to this novel (Wegs 217). It too has within it contradictory implications that make it particularly applicable to Milkman. Icarus and his father, Daedalus, fly to seek freedom from the Labyrinth in which they have been placed by Theseus. Daedalus makes the wings for Icarus, and he warns him of the dangers of flying too close to the sun. The self-exaltation of flight causes Icarus to disregard these warnings (Hamilton 193). Thus, though Icarus flies to seek freedom, it is ultimately the self-exaltation of flight that causes him to disregard his father's warning and fly too close to the sun. Milkman goes to the South to escape his life at home. And though he is not taught to fly by his father, the person he emulates in flight is his great-grandfather. Furthermore, like those of Icarus, Milkman's motives are mixed.

Milkman comes to the South seeking gold. While there, he discovers the legends associated with his past. But still he is exhilarated by the whole idea of his great-grandfather's flying. His ecstatic speech to Sweet is very much a celebration of the individuality of his great-grandfather, the Icarus-like exaltation of his flight: "'You hear that? Guitar, my great-granddaddy could flyyyyyy and the whole damn town is named after him. Tell him, Sweet'" (328). Milkman's exultation is so complete that he fails to grasp the significance of Sweet's question: "'Who'd he leave behind?'" (328). However, when he gets to Pilate's house, anxious to enlighten her on the past, she breaks a wine bottle over his head and leaves him in the cellar. This incident makes it clear that Milkman must integrate what he has learned about the past with the life that he has lived. He must look inward and understand himself as well as those who lived before him. He must see the relationship between his great-grandfather's life and his own. Just as his great-grandfather flew away leaving a woman who grieved herself to death, so did Milkman. Appropriately, while in the cellar, he figures out the reason for Pilate's anger, and he recognizes the person he left behind. Pilate is angry because Hagar is dead, and Milkman must accept some responsibility for Hagar's death. Thus, when Milkman returns to Shalimar with Pilate, he carries with him a box of Hagar's hair, a symbol of the person he left behind. But the final scene of the novel becomes not a celebration of Milkman, the supposed hero of this novel, but rather a re-examination of the very scene he is re-enacting: the flight of Solomon.

Just as Morrison has shown us that words must be reclaimed if they are to become one's own, so here she shows us that this whole legend must be re-examined. The central figure becomes Pilate, and the legend of flight is consistently undercut. Pilate's dying request that Milkman sing brings from him the song about his great-grandfather, but now Pilate becomes the central character in the song: "Sugargirl don't leave me here" (336). The words have been reclaimed, for now they apply not to the heroic flight of legendary man, but to the life of an heroic woman, a woman who did not fly away. Milkman recognizes Pilate's true measure, a heroism that contrasts sharply to that of his great-grandfather: "Without ever leaving the ground she could fly" (336). When Milkman wonders if there is another like her, he is placing her in the rarefied position of the legendary figure, the hero or heroine of songs and stories, the one who is celebrated for his or her uniqueness. Finally, Pilate's own last words contrast sharply with Milkman's great-grandfather's legendary act. She tells Milkman to watch Reba and then she says "'I wish I'd a knowed more people. I would have loved em all'" (336). In flying away, Solomon left Ryna to watch his offspring. Furthermore, the very selfishness of his act—seeking freedom for himself—contrasts sharply with

Pilate's community ethic: to know and love as many people as possible. Within the context of Pilate's dying words, it is hard to see Milkman's flight as entirely heroic. He does leave the ground to fly. But whether he is seeking Guitar's arms to avenge the death of Pilate or simply to confront the inevitable, he is already disobeying Pilate's admonition of love and forgetting her request that he watch Reba. Thus, in some respects, Milkman is repeating the mistakes of his great-grandfather.

Morrison has addressed this very issue in an interview. She ties Milkman's flight to the propensity of black men to travel: "it is a part of black life, a positive, majestic thing, but there is a price to pay—the price is the children" (Holloway and Demetrako-poulos 87). Morrison is calling attention to the tension that we find in the last scene in the novel: tension between flying away and staying on the ground. Milkman's flight fulfills his destiny. He is the hero; he has been initiated and has discovered the importance of his past. Moreover, he has longed for flight since he was a child. Pilate told his mother the day before his birth, "'A little bird'll be here with the morning'" (9). Thus, Milkman is supposed to fly; it is, in Morrison's words, "positive, majestic." But Morrison will not let us focus on Milkman's heroism without forcing us to be aware of the heroine who stays on the ground. This tension is reflected in the inscription at the beginning of the novel: "The fathers may soar/ And the children may know their names." In many respects this is exactly what happens in the novel. Solomon does fly, and the children celebrate him in song; they know his name. But there is another sense in which the inscription exposes the tension. The children do not know any more than his name: they do not know him as a father, as an ancestor. Moreover, there is some doubt about what his name is: Susan Byrd tells Milkman, "'Solomon or Shalimar—I never knew which was right'" (322). Milkman's family does not know either name. It must be reconstructed. But even in the reconstruction, there is a problem of emphasis. Milkman remembers Solomon's flight, but he forgets those Solomon left on the ground; he sees the foreground of the picture and not the background. In similar fashion, we are tempted to see Milkman as the hero of this novel because he flies, and to forget Pilate who flies "without ever leaving the ground" (336). In the novel as a whole, we tend to see Pilate as the background, and Milkman as the foreground. But Morrison insists that we see both, indeed that we reverse them so that Pilate becomes foreground and Milkman background. Thus, the title of the novel may be read in two ways. Solomon's song is about Solomon, but in the end it is also about Pilate.

In a larger sense this novel is about more than any one character. Foreground and background also apply to the relation that Milkman discovers between history and his ancestors. As Milkman seeks his name, the name of his ancestors, he must look beneath the historical record: "Under the recorded names were other names, just as 'Macon Dead,' recorded for all time in some dusty file, hid from view the real names of people, places, and things. Names that had meaning" (329). Once again the struggle is over words. The remembered names are those that the official language recognizes: Doctor Street is officially Mains Avenue. Finding the reality behind those names, the names in the background, is the task of those who were left out. Once again, we see the struggle to make the word one's own. So it is fitting that Morrison should place this story in the midst of landscapes familiar to readers of American fiction. It is a novel that re-enacts and undercuts traditional patterns within that fiction. The struggle for language is the struggle for social grounding, for empowerment.

In *Playing in the Dark* Morrison identifies "autonomy" and "absolute power" as major themes of American literature. But she argues that these concepts were given other names by historians and critics, by writers themselves, much in the same way that No

Mercy Hospital was called a charity hospital. According to Morrison, "autonomy" was called "individualism"; "absolute power" was called "a romantic, conquering 'heroism'" (44-45). This novel explores the limits of heroism and the limits of individualism. For every hero who flies, there is someone who waits on the ground, and for every individual who fully develops himself or herself, who stands clearly in the foreground, there is someone who stands in the background. For Milkman it was Hagar, Pilate, and Ruth. For Macon it was Ruth and before her Pilate. Macon acknowledges indebtedness to no one; Milkman is similar until very late in the novel. Each of them is solitary, and in that respect they are acting upon very American assumptions: that there can be no limit placed upon the individual's right to develop himself, that the hero stands alone against the wilderness. Each of these men feels constrained by those around him. Milkman realizes late in the novel that he owes his very life to Ruth and Pilate but that "he had never so much as made either of them a cup of tea" (331). He also recognizes too late his indebtedness to Hagar. He cannot escape responsibility for her death. Macon ruthlessly collects his rent, making homeless those who cannot pay, just as the Butlers left him and Pilate homeless. He literally feeds on the community of blacks within which he lives. Each of these men ignores the background of the picture. Milkman discovers the complexities of flying away: that flight can be an evasion as much as an act of courage. He also discovers the subversions of language: that for every one whose name lives, there is someone whose name has been covered over, arbitrarily made "dead," whether by the oppressive force of history or the selective nature of memory. Furthermore, whole cultures die when they are forced to live in the shadows, forced to be the background of the picture. American individualism was in some respects bought with black enslavement. As Morrison says in *Playing in the Dark*,

What was distinctive about the New [World] was, first of all, its claim to freedom and, second, the presence of the unfree within the heart of the democratic experiment—the critical absence of democracy, its echo, shadow, and silent force in the political and intellectual activity of some not Americans. (48)

This novel explores the shadow, both in the historical record and in the songs and legends of black culture; it brings it forth into the light.

It is thus appropriate that Milkman should be a young man who rediscovers his roots in the agrarian world of Shalimar, that he should stand on the very land that his grandfather named Lincoln's Heaven, for in the context of this novel that land becomes an important emblem. In order to see that land as anything more than a repository for gold, Milkman must lose the accumulated weight of his past, much in the spirit of Ike McCaslin and the narrator of *Walden*. But even after he has understood the land as an emblem of his heritage, he still must struggle to make sense of the stories enfolded in it. That land is a symbol of his great-grandfather's self-sufficiency and independence. But it is also a symbol of his great-grandfather's indebtedness to those around him. There is no independence either for Milkman or for those first settlers who farmed that land, for they all relied on others. Milkman relied on Pilate and Ruth and Hagar; those first settlers relied on the slaves they brought with them.

In such a context *Song of Solomon* itself becomes a novel that at once embraces and undercuts mainstream traditions. Lincoln's Heaven is destroyed by the Butlers; it ultimately brings forth Macon Dead and his greedy lifestyle. So paradise is spoiled by greed, development, the machine inevitably a part of the garden. But it also produces Pilate. She demonstrates her respect for the landscape by her habit of keeping a rock from every place she has lived and by reading forever her grade-school geography book. Despite being run out of Shalimar and numerous other places, she carries the bones of her ancestor with her, acknowledging thereby her indebtedness to those who came before her. Ultimately, she is rooted in the landscape her father saw as paradise, dying on land named for her ancestors. Milkman is consistently presented to us as the hero who comes of age, the young man who discovers his roots. But in the act of fulfilling his destiny, re-enacting his grandfather's flight, he recognizes Pilate's subtle heroism: she flies without leaving the ground. Indeed, he becomes the one to sing the song about her, just as the children sing the song of Solomon, just as Ryna might have sung to Solomon. Whatever his final end, he has recognized for a moment the importance of those around him. And we as readers have seen the background of the picture, not the hero coming of age, but those who made it possible for him to come of age.

Both of Morrison's first novels focus upon the absence of viable mainstream traditions for black culture. Each of these novels focuses upon the tension that exists between black and white universes, worlds cut off and separated from one another. *Song of Solomon* is different, for it merges these two universes. Mainstream traditions are re-examined, transformed.

Keith Byerman says of the blues and folktales of black culture that such forms consistently imply that any type of trouble is "both personal and communal" (57). Such is what Morrison suggests here. Men are not solitary fliers, nor are white Americans solitary settlers. But at the same time, the act of flying is, in Morrison's words, "glorious," and Morrison is not interested in denying that. She is also not interested in denying that Lincoln's Heaven was a kind of paradise. Rather, Morrison is interested in completing what has been a partial picture, in bringing into the light what has been in the shadows. In many respects *Song of Solomon* is a turning point and an ending for Morrison. The first two novels reject mainstream traditions: the primer version of reality, the uncomprehending visitors from Medallion. In contrast, *Song of Solomon* explores mainstream traditions. But Morrison does not see these traditions as ends in themselves, for in the next half of her career she moves beyond them.

Notes

1. Campbell's description of this process is as follows: "A hero ventures forth from the world of common day into a region of supernatural wonder: fabulous forces are there encountered and a decisive victory is won: the hero comes back from this mysterious adventure with the power to bestow boons on his fellow man" (30).

2. For a good discussion of this pattern see the article by Cynthia Davis, "Self, Society, and Myth in Toni Morrison's Fiction," Toni Morrison: *Modern Critical Views* (New York: Chelsea House, 1990).

3. In his book *Inspiriting Influences* (New York: Columbia, 1989) Michael Awkward uses portions of this passage to support and define what he calls denigration, the way in which African-American female writers transform western cultural and expressive traditions.

FIVE

Tar Baby:

Lost Connections

Tar Baby is in many respects a complete departure from Morrison's earlier work. Most of the action takes place outside of the United States. Moreover, the characters are unlike those in the earlier novels. Half of them are wealthy white aristocrats. The other half are black, but even these characters are in some respects unique in Morrison's work. Thérèse is a black native of Dominique. Gideon is an American who has taken residence in Dominique. Ondine and Sidney are transplanted Philadelphians, members of the servant class. Jadine, though, is Morrison's first portrayal of a young, modern, educated black woman. She has all of the monetary advantages of white society, those things that Pecola and Sula lack, and many of the choices she makes reflect her orientation toward bourgeois culture. She is educated in art history, she prefers Picasso to "an Itumba mask" (74), and her face has appeared on the covers of various European fashion magazines. Even Son, whose outlaw status reminds us of Cholly Breedlove, Sula, and Guitar, has qualities that set him apart from Morrison's earlier characters. With his dredlocks and his resplendently black skin, he is more self-consciously black than any of Morrison's earlier characters. Moreover, he reverses the pattern of *Song of Solomon*. Instead of the man who leaves, he becomes the man who follows, for at the end of the novel, it is he who seeks Jadine, helplessly drawn to her beauty, despite all that he despises about the choices she makes.

This novel is also different from the earlier novels because its focus is unremittingly on relationships among people of varying colors. Morrison's earlier novels have dealt in part with human relationships: family relationships in *The Bluest Eye*; friendship and community in *Sula* and *Song of Solomon*. But never before has Morrison focused so intensely on romantic relationships (Jade and Son) or upon the relationship between master and servant (the Streets and the Childs). Never before has she examined so carefully the role that color plays in these relationships. Furthermore, this emphasis within the novel is closely tied to Morrison's choice of settings. Most of the characters are separated from their homes; thus, they are dependent upon one another in a way that they would not be in more familiar territory.

Still, there are some similarities between this novel and Morrison's earlier work. The narrative voice in this novel reminds us of what we saw in *The Bluest Eye* and *Sula*, for the perspective shifts repeatedly. We move into the minds and into the background of practically every character in the novel. Some passages even take us into the consciousness of the daisy trees and the butterflies. More importantly, the use of allusions in this novel reminds us of *Song of Solomon*. Here, just as in *Song of Solomon*, Morrison uses allusion to undercut and question Western assumptions and traditions.

The most prominent allusion is in the title of the novel: Tar Baby. Once again we see Morrison alluding to complicated myth and legend. The tar baby story is as many-faceted and as varied as the stories of the flying Africans. Even though this may be the most significant allusion in this novel, it is certainly not the only one. The novel begins with an allusion to Conrad's story "The Secret Sharer." Both works focus upon a stowaway whose presence transforms those around him. Morrison has repeatedly emphasized her desire to write a literature that challenges the traditions of the West. The allusion to Conrad allows her to do just that, for Morrison uses the tar baby story to challenge the assumptions implicit in Conrad's story. This work presents the reader with what Bakhtin calls "multiple languages"; Conrad's story presents one language and the tar baby story another. According to Bakhtin, each language within a novel represents an "ideological belief system" (*Dialogic* 311). Furthermore, in the course of the novel, these systems "are unmasked and destroyed as something false, hypocritical, greedy, limited, narrowly rationalistic, inadequate to reality" (312). In *Tar Baby*, Morrison "unmasks" the language of the Conrad story in much the way Bakhtin describes. This "unmasking" will be the main concern of this chapter.

Morrison has argued in *Playing in the Dark* and her essay "Unspeakable Things Unspoken" that the Eurocentric tradition has always used a language that contained an African presence, even when that presence was not acknowledged. Both *Playing in the Dark* and "Unspeakable Things Unspoken" explore this dimension of American literature. But the broad tradition that she examines in both of these works is European in origin. Calling this tradition "Africanism," Morrison states,

> As a disabling virus within literary discourse, Africanism has become, in the European tradition that American education favors, both a way of talking about and a way of policing matters of class, sexual license, and repression, formations and exercises of power, and meditations on ethics and accountability. (*Playing* 7)

Furthermore, she makes clear that her term refers to a misunderstanding of African people: "I use the term for the denotative and connotative blackness that African people have come to signify, as well as the entire range of views, assumptions, readings, and misreadings that accompany Eurocentric learning about these people" (7). Thus, according to Morrison, there is within the European tradition a tacit agreement that certain literary figurations signal the presence of Africanism, despite the presence or absence of black characters. Moreover, these figurations carry with them a clearly defined set of values. Darkness is associated with the side of the self that one represses, the side of the self that is uncivilized, wild, savage. Coding such concepts with color implies that they are connected with certain races. According to such a system, the black African is by nature savage, wild, uncivilized. In contrast, the white European is tame, restrained, and civilized. Moreover, the value system associated with these colors operates independently of specific black and white characters. For example, the darkness of the islands in Conrad's "The Secret Sharer" implies that they are uncivilized and wild.

White writers often confront Africanism in oblique ways. Morrison analyzes *Moby Dick* in "Unspeakable Things Unspoken." The whiteness of the whale becomes for Morrison not an emblem of ambiguity as it is for most critics but rather a representation of ideology: the unremitting whiteness that will admit of no tinge of blackness. The whale becomes a metaphor for a society that recognizes nothing outside of its own color, a society that is by nature not just segregated but unaware of its own savagery (214).[1] Since white is all this culture sees, anything that is black is simply absent, not a part of civilization.

Awareness is the central subject of Conrad's "The Secret Sharer." A ship captain on his first command, the narrator of the story is unaware of himself and of his ship. Early in the story he tells us, "But what I felt most was my being a stranger on the ship; and if all the truth must be told, I was somewhat of a stranger to myself" (650). His meeting with Leggatt, the "secret sharer," is presented in images of darkness and light. The man's body "flickered in the sleeping water with the elusive, silent play of summer lightning in a night sky" (654). Leggatt's actions have been judged by the captain and the crew of the *Sephora* to be savage, uncivilized. He has strangled a man in rage, and he accepts society's judgment concerning the matter, alluding to Cain, a figure who has been associated with the black race: "'What does the Bible say? 'Driven off the face of the earth.' Very well, I am off the face of the earth now. As I came at night so I shall go'" (688). Thus, Leggatt comes to symbolize all of those things that the narrator does not know about himself and all of those things that Conrad's society would associate with darkness: savagery, rage, the breakdown of law. But ironically, as the title of the story implies, in coming to know Leggatt, the narrator comes to know himself and his ship. Leggatt is a secret self, a self that is a dimension of darkness. As if to prove this, Leggatt leaves in darkness. Koh-ring, the island which he is left to swim to, is described in these terms: "Unknown to trade, to travel, almost to geography, the manner of life they [Koh-ring and the islands around it] harbor is an unsolved secret" (689). As the ship moves closer to the island, the narrator emphasizes its darkness; indeed it is almost a darkness to be likened to Moby Dick's whiteness: "The black southern hill of Koh-ring seemed to hang right over the ship like a towering fragment of the everlasting night. On that enormous mass of blackness there was not a gleam to be seen, not a sound to be heard" (695). Later the narrator tells us that his fate and his ship's hang in the balance as he commands the crew to take the craft to its very edge, "the gate of everlasting night" (698). After this encounter with darkness, both human and inhuman, the narrator feels that he knows himself and knows his ship: "no one in the world would stand between us" (699). Conrad suggests that fully knowing the self involves an understanding of darkness, savagery, the parts of the self that are uncharted. Conrad's narrator repeatedly describes these character traits in images of darkness.

Allusions to "The Secret Sharer" begin on the first page of *Tar Baby*. In the darkness of night, Son leaves the H.M.S. *Stor Konigsgaarten* and becomes a stowaway on the yatch the Streets use. Several factors tie him to Conrad's Leggatt. Like Leggatt, he is a refugee from civilization and from the law. He has run and hidden for eight years and in that time he has had "seven documented identities and before that a few undocumented ones" (139). Moreover, like Leggatt he has killed a person in a fit of rage: his former wife Cheyenne. Also, like Leggatt, he is attempting to get to an island. *Tar Baby* begins and ends with Son's attempts in the darkness of night to approach an island. At the beginning of the novel, he approaches Queen of France. Morrison's narrator tells us that the current will not let him close to the island: "Like the hand of an insistent woman it pushed him" (4). To get there and into Valerian's house, he must board the *Seabird II*. At the end of the novel he approaches Isle de Chevalier by boat, but though he reaches shore this time, we do not know where he will go: into the darkness to seek the mythical blind slaves or to the Streets to look for Jadine. In short, like Leggatt he moves out of the unknown into the unknown.

As Leggatt is identified with the secret self of the narrator of "The Secret Sharer," so Son is identified with the secret selves of many of the characters in *Tar Baby*. To Thérèse, he is a visitor from the realm of myth, "a horseman come down here to get her [Jadine]" (107). Valerian allows him to stay at the house because in Son's presence Valerian has a vision of Michael, his own son, and thinks that Michael would approve. Son has bizarre effects upon Valerian's greenhouse; it is almost as if he knows the secret selves of the plants. He shakes the cyclamen stems and causes it to bloom. A day later the hydrangea blooms. Finally, Son forces the five main characters into contact with long repressed dimensions of themselves. His presence forces Sidney and Ondine to begin to question their roles. His presence at Christmas dinner causes Ondine and Margaret to confront the abuse of Michael, their long- held secret. This revelation, in turn, forces Valerian to discover unknown dimensions of Margaret. Valerian ultimately sees that his wife is not an alcoholic; rather she is an abusive mother. Moreover, he discerns his involvement in the loss of his son's love and respect. The central focus of the novel is Son's effect upon Jadine: "He had jangled something in her that was so repulsive, so awful, and he had managed to make her feel that the thing that repelled her was not in him, but in her" (123). Thus, Son is a kind of Leggatt, one whose presence forces those on the island to confront the unknown in themselves and in those around them.

But more important than the similarities between "The Secret Sharer" and *Tar Baby* are the differences. The most obvious difference is perspective. Conrad's story is told from the vantage point of the ship captain, not the stow away. In fact, throughout the story, we see only the captain's understanding of Leggatt and Leggatt's effect upon him. Morrison's novel contains so many shifts in perspective that we see most of the characters from various angles. But the novel begins and ends with Son's vantage point. He is the outsider. Thus, the perspective that Morrison often uses in this novel is the opposite of that which Conrad uses.

Also, in many respects, Morrison's story undercuts the clean resolution of Conrad's story. Leggatt brings to the narrator of "The Secret Sharer" a confrontation that is ultimately positive. The narrator comes to know a kind of darkness in this confrontation and as a result comes to trust himself more fully and thus to trust and know his ship. We end the story with "the perfect communion of a seaman with his first command" and the secret sharer swimming away "a free man, a proud swimmer striking out for a new destiny" (699). At the end of *Tar Baby*, there is a pronounced lack of harmony. Jadine and Son have parted company, each a kind of orphan unable to communicate with one another. Son cannot be a part of Eloe, nor can he be apart from it. Similarly, Jadine cannot separate herself from New York and Europe, nor can she be a part of them and be "unorphaned" by Son. But Jadine is orphaned in other ways also; she has cut herself off from Ondine and Sidney. Furthermore, Valerian and Margaret now know the truth about one another; rather than bringing them together or making them independent, it has driven them apart and made Valerian more dependent than ever upon Ondine and Sidney. To Margaret, he is a kind of child. In short, though Son is a kind of Leggatt to many members of the Street household, the ultimate cost of self- knowledge is not harmony but disharmony. The characters in *Tar Baby* have little success in coming to know and accept their inner selves. In short, in many respects this novel directly challenges the assumptions implied by Conrad's story.

The contrast to *Song of Solomon* is also significant. That novel moves toward resolution and wholeness through reclamation; this novel moves away from resolution. But this novel broadens Morrison's perspective, for she deals here with a large array of characters. In the first three novels white characters appear on the horizon: the white family that Pauline Breedlove works for in *The Bluest Eye*, the white citizens who visit the Bottom in *Sula*, the Butlers in *Song of Solomon*, the white citizens who insist that Doctor Street be Mains Avenue. But in *Tar Baby* for the first time Morrison makes white characters central. She enters their minds just as she does those of black characters. And all of these characters—black and white—share one perception: they all see in Son a kind of savagery that they associate with color. In this respect they conform to the pattern Morrison sets forth in *Playing in the Dark*: they see the uncivilized and the unknown as black. This is also the pattern that we see at work in Conrad's story.

When Margaret finds Son in her closet, her fear makes her incoherent. The one word that she can manage is "Black" (79). Margaret, Ondine, and Sidney also call him a "nigger" at one point or another, a word that by its very nature codes color with savagery. Margaret calls him a "gorilla" in front of Jadine (129); to herself she says that he is "literally, literally a nigger in the woodpile" (83). Jadine calls him an "ape" and a "nigger" when he makes sexual advances toward her (121). Sidney says to Ondine "If that nigger wants to steal something or kill somebody you think he's going to skip us just 'cause we don't own it?" (99). To all of these black and white characters, Son represents the unknown and the uncivilized, and the language they use to describe him shows that they associate these characteristics with his blackness.

Jadine's first encounter with Son by herself makes clear that she sees animal-like qualities in him also. First, she notices his smell. Then she sees him in the mirror into which she stares. His hair is "overpowering—physically overpowering" (113). Jadine reflects upon it as "long whips or lashes that could grab her and beat her to jelly" (113). Later she thinks of it as "wild, aggressive, vicious hair.... Uncivilized, reform school hair...., chain-gang hair" (113). But there is an important irony in this scene.

While Jadine notices the uncivilized in Son, she is almost completely unaware of the same qualities in herself. Once again Son is affecting a "secret self" in Jadine. Morrison repeatedly describes this side of Jadine as "small dark dogs galloping on silver feet" (113). In Son's presence, Jadine is constantly trying to control the dogs because he attracts her. More important to this particular scene are the mirror and the coat. Jadine stands before the mirror looking at herself in a black and white sealskin coat, a gift from her European lover. She notices Son in the mirror, reflecting on his "chain gang hair," but she never notices the savagery the coat she wears represents. It is made from the skins of ninety baby seals, each of which was brutally clubbed to death. Moreover, it represents the savagery and power of European civilization, for it is an artifact of bourgeois culture, not African culture. By wearing the coat Jadine participates in the savagery of that culture. But though she looks in the mirror, she does not see such savagery in herself; she sees it in Son.

In many respects, the other main characters in the novel have the same reaction to Son that Jadine initially does: they see in him a savagery that they fail to acknowledge in themselves. This lack of insight is particularly true of Valerian and Margaret. Similar to the narrator of "The Secret Sharer," they lack awareness and self-knowledge. Thus, the meeting with Son becomes a confrontation with darkness, the other, the unknown. Margaret is the character who is most horrified by Son's presence. His having been in her closet causes her to think of it "as a toilet where something rotten had been and still was" (86). After fantasizing that Son might have masturbated there, Margaret decides to throw away all of her clothes and buy new ones. However, the darkness in her closet is not Son at all; rather it is her abuse of her own son, Michael. The entire focus of her activities in the first half of the novel is Michael's Christmas visit, an attempt to reclaim the affection that she lost by abusing him. When her secret abuse of Michael is revealed at the dinner table, her response is again to refuse to see what is inside her, to refuse to look into the closet of herself: "'I have always loved my son,'…. 'I am not one of those women in the *National Enquirer*.'" Margaret's statement shows that she is "policing" matters of class, to use Morrison's term. Just as Son's blackness makes her closet into a "toilet," so the acknowledgment of her abuse of Michael threatens to destroy her social position. Thus, she clings to a detail to separate herself from those she considers common, the women who appear in the *National Enquirer*: she loves her child while she beats him; they do not. Her social position protects her from the blackness of Son and the vulgarity of the women in the *National Enquirer*.

Valerian's lack of awareness is also pointed. Though he is tolerant of, even amused by Son's presence, his tolerance vanishes when at Christmas dinner Son questions his firing of Gideon and

Thérèse. Valerian responds with disdain: "'Surely you don't expect me to explain my actions, defend them to you?'" (205). Son understands Valerian's debt to those around him, his "secret." Valerian's wealth came at the expense of the very natives whom he now employs and fires with a cavalier flourish of the hand. Son characterizes this as behavior unfit for an animal: "they [Valerian and those like him] had not the dignity of wild animals who did not eat where they defecated but they could defecate over a whole people and come there to live and defecate some more" (203). As the meal progresses, Valerian's blind spots become even more obvious. Ondine tells him "'I may be a cook, Mr. Street, but I'm a person too'" (207). And fittingly Ondine shows what a person she is: it was she who protected and defended Michael from his mother's abuse. Such a reversal is important, for it goes against the color code. Margaret, who has sugary white skin, is the brutal one in this case; though treated as less than a person, Ondine shows herself to be more human than those who employ her. Thus, Valerian must come to terms with his indebtedness to Ondine, but also with his wife's true nature and with his own nature, which up until now has been hidden in a closet. Valerian's weakness has always been a lack of awareness: "he had not taken the trouble to know" (242). Much like the narrator of "The Secret Sharer," he has not known himself. Valerian's ultimate condemnation of himself could apply to every character in his household: "No man should live without absorbing the sins of his kind" (243). In projecting their sins on the dark skin of Son and people like him (Yardman and the Marys, people whose names they hardly know), these characters have avoided self-knowledge. And now they pay the price. They have projected on blackness all that they feared and did not know about themselves; now they find the tar all over themselves that blackened others. Thus, the allusion to tar baby in the title of the novel is important. Ultimately, it becomes the vehicle through which Morrison challenges the assumptions implied by Conrad's story.

The allusion to the tar baby story in the title of this novel is many faceted. There are numerous references to tar in the story that have nothing to do with Brer Rabbit, Uncle Remus, or the tar baby tales. As Dorothy Lee argues "It seems a mistake to force the tale too closely on the novel, for the words 'tar baby' function primarily to suggest Black identity in a more general sense" (355). Though Lee may overstate the case, she does bring up a significant point: tar serves as a metaphor for blackness in this story. In his nightly visits to Jadine's room, Son hopes "to breathe into her the smell of tar and its shiny consistency" (120). When she sinks in the swamp, the mud that coats her body "looks like pitch" according to Margaret (185). While she sinks, she encounters the mythical swamp women who represent her cultural roots. The woman in yellow who fascinates and terrifies Jadine has "skin like tar" (45). She too has a mythical quality: she carries eggs and functions as a symbol of black womanhood. In all of these instances tar symbolizes the blackness that Jadine lacks. And in many respects, Morrison has reversed the color coding that is so prominent in the Streets' response to Son. Just as his blackness makes Son frightening to Margaret when she first sees him, so Jadine's light coloring causes Son to distrust her when he first sees her. He is trapped by her beauty, but while she sleeps he hopes to make her black, to fill her with dreams of tar.

Other characters also respond negatively to Jade because she is not black enough. Gideon calls her a "yalla" and tells Son that it is hard for her "not to be white people" (155). In similar fashion, Thérèse sees Jadine as someone who needs rescuing and later judges her as one who has "forgotten her ancient properties" (305). There is a degree of truth to all of these accusations. Jadine is tied inextricably to white culture by money and upbringing. But there is also an implied judgment on the parts of characters such as Son, Thérèse, and Gideon: that blackness is a particular set of responses. Elliott Butler-Evans argues that evaluations of Jadine often go awry when they ignore a central issue confronting black women: their need "to construct their own identities without having to submit to a dominant myth of racial authenticity" (157). Jadine certainly feels the pull of the swamp women; she feels the power of Son's black skin. But she must ultimately integrate these forces into the more immediate parts of her background: New York City, Paris, and her career. Her choice to abandon Son, Sidney, and Ondine means that she cannot, and thus she becomes one more of the divided selves in the novel. But significantly her failure is precisely that of the other characters: she fails in her search for awareness. She cannot integrate the secret self that the swamp women and the woman in yellow represent, the self that Son "jangles" loose, with the self that appears on the pages of fashion magazines. Thus, her relationship to Son is doomed to failure.

The tar baby story has interesting applications to Jadine's situation. If we interpret the story from Son's vantage point, she is the tar baby. In fact, Son tells the story to her in one of their last encounters, identifying her as the tar baby and Valerian as the white farmer. In this reading of the story, she is the construct of white culture, and her devastating beauty allows her to pull Son away from his life of exile and also away from his past in Eloe. But such a reading ignores the complexity of Jadine's situation. She too is pulled away from her normal activities by his blackness. He is the construct of black society, and for her he is irresistible. But modeling and Eloe do not mix, and Son ultimately refuses to conform to what he finds in New York City. Thus, the relationship ends. But whereas we never learn whether Son finds the briar patch, we may assume that Jadine does. At the end of the novel she has returned to the lifestyle she led at the beginning. It is unauthentic, commercialized, and perhaps misdirected, but it does allow her to escape the tar that Son has breathed into her. Further, it is what she was born and bred to, much as Brer Rabbit was born and bred in a briar patch.

The tar baby story has broader implications in this novel. Brer Rabbit is a member of the trickster tradition which stretches far back into African culture. According to John Roberts, a central emphasis within the tradition is the making and breaking of social ties for material gain (103). According to such a measure, every character in *Tar Baby* would be a potential Brer Rabbit. Valerian has made his tie with the Caribbean island for material gain. He earned his money by harvesting sugar grown on the island; he built his home amid its beauty. But both processes destroyed the environment. Indeed the plants that he grows in his greenhouse stand in sharp contrast to those he destroyed as he built upon the island. In marrying Valerian, Margaret broke ties with her poverty stricken home: she became a sort of orphan because the money was right. She hates Isles de Chevalier, but she stays there because of Valerian. Sidney and Ondine have nothing of their own that does not come from Valerian. Throughout the novel they are torn between their own feelings—Ondine's hatred of Margaret, Sidney's anger at Valerian for allowing Son to stay—and their need for job security. It is job security—the material tie—that wins out.

Jadine's breaking of ties is pronounced throughout the novel. She is educated through Sidney and Ondine and their ties to Valerian. She breaks with them to come to New York with Son; but when he refuses to get an education and become a lawyer, she goes back to her Paris boyfriend, a man wealthy enough to buy her a sealskin coat. What is more, in going to Paris, she leaves Ondine and Sidney to work out their own problems.

Son is also a kind of Brer Rabbit. He steals food from Valerian; then when he is caught, he is initially able to play the part of the penitent so that he may stay and eat some more. In some respects, even after his departure from the Streets, he is living off Jadine's income. Even Thérèse and Gideon would fit into this category. To work for Valerian, they play parts. Gideon pretends that he cannot read. Thérèse changes identities frequently—she is one of several Marys. And though she hates all of the Street household, she does not show her feeling until she is fired for stealing apples. Instead, she merely avoids looking at them. Thus, in some respects all of these characters are Brer Rabbits, playing a part in order to get what they need.

Trudier Harris states in her book *Fiction and Folklore* that despite the Uncle Remus tradition, the Brer Rabbit of African folklore is usually female (119) and that despite Morrison's emphasis on the sexual relationship between Son and Jadine, "sex is not the usual objective of the trickster" (123). He or she seeks to survive. Survival skills are precisely what we see in each of these characters with the exception of Son. They all do what they have to do to maintain their lifestyles. Only Son at the beginning of the novel is risking survival in pursuit of something other than food. In the first part of the novel, he is presumably seeking freedom. He becomes entangled in the Street household because he needs to eat (much like Brer Rabbit); then he sees Jadine and falls in love. At the end of the novel he is no longer seeking food; he is seeking Jadine. And in the process he has lost his freedom. Thus, there is pronounced irony in the first line of the novel: "He believed he was safe" (3). Morrison seems to suggest in this novel that no one is safe because survival always has a cost.

In the African-American version of the tar baby story, the main issue is power. The person who contends with Brer Rabbit (whether he be Brer Fox or the white farmer) is a power figure. Thus, Brer Rabbit must use his wits for survival (Roberts 108; 112). In that respect this novel becomes a portrait of a struggle for survival in the world of the Streets. Each of the black characters uses a different device for survival. Gideon pretends to be illiterate. Thérèse does not look the Streets or the Childs in the face. Sidney is proud of his history of survival: "he became one of those industrious Philadelphia Negroes—the proudest people in the race" (61). He tells Son, "'You had a job, you chucked it.... I am a Phil-a-delphia Negro mentioned in the book of the very same name. My people owned drugstores and taught school while yours were still cutting their faces open so as to be able to tell one of you from the other'" (163). The point here is that survival comes first—before freedom, before racial pride, before anything. Ondine concurs with Sidney on this point, for it is she who calms Sidney down when he becomes angry with Valerian for allowing Son to stay: "'Keep on and you'll have us over in them shacks in Queen of France'" (101). Even after Ondine erupts into rage at Margaret at the Christmas dinner, survival is still an issue for Ondine and Sidney. The next morning before the dishes are cleared, Sidney is asking Valerian, "'You going to let us go?'" (233). Even Jadine, whom the other black characters see as nearly white, survives among whites through a carefully concocted strategy: "She needed only to be stunning, and to convince them [the whites] she was not as smart as they were" (127). In fact, despite the distrust which many black characters have for her, Jadine sees her motives as nearly identical to that of all the blacks around her except Son: "the black people she knew wanted what she wanted.... whatever their scam, 'making it' was on their minds and they played the game with house cards, each deck issued and dealt by the house" (126). The "house card" are those issued by Valerian, the very "deck" that Son calls into question at Christmas dinner.

But the ending of *Tar Baby* casts serious doubt upon Valerian's power to deal cards and run houses.[2] He is still the center of attention at the end of the novel, but Jadine notes upon her return that Margaret talks about Valerian as if he were a child (283). Others must tell him when to get a haircut. Sidney feeds him and opens his mail. What is more, the last time we see Valerian,

Sidney seems to be tacitly in charge. He drinks Valerian's wine despite his master's protest; he tells him of the family's plans. Valerian says that the family will soon be leaving Isle de Chevalier, but Sidney says "'I figure we're going to be here a long time, Mr. Street'" (287). Valerian observes that something is wrong: "'Something's happening here'" (287). But when Sidney starts the music, he relaxes and smiles. Once again we hear an echo of the tar baby story: Brer Rabbit does not have financial power. He must eat in the master's garden or starve. Thus, metaphorically, he is stuck in the master's tar. But ultimately Brer Rabbit does survive because he tricks the master. He gives his master the illusion of authority, while he keeps for himself the power to make decisions. In short, Valerian has been deposed.

By tying this story to the trickster tradition, by insisting that each character has a dimension of Brer Rabbit in him or her, Morrison consistently undercuts Conrad's "The Secret Sharer." That story suggests to us that the self is knowable, that the darkness contains a man who looks just like the hero, only he is clothed in shadows. This novel moves toward no easy resolution. For even when these characters look into the darkness of their closets, they refuse to accept what they find. In addition, interpersonal relationships are a series of tricks played for material gain with the ultimate goal always being survival. Thus, the language of Conrad's story is unmasked: darkness, self, and friendship all take on new meanings in the world Morrison creates. And Conrad's language—what Bakhtin would call his "socio-ideological belief system"—is shown to be inadequate.

In *The Signifying Monkey*, Henry Louis Gates attempts to establish a theoretical underpinning for an approach to black literature. In so doing, he explores two figures from African mythology: Esu and Ifa. Ifa is the god of determinate meanings; Esu is the god of indeterminate, figurative meanings. Gates argues that the tension between these two figures is reflected in the

double-voiced discourse so commonly found in black literature.
Such a tension is evident in the allusions that Morrison uses here.
Conrad provides us with a self whose secrets are knowable. We
might see in such a depiction an echo of Ifa, the god of determinate meanings. Morrison's novel undercuts the certainty of
Conrad's story, for everywhere we look there are deception and
manipulation; the self has no conclusion. It is an Esu, constantly
evolving.

In one of the most well-known Esu stories, Esu wears a hat
that is white on one side and black on the other. He passes a
crowd of people from one side and then turns and passes from the
other side. The crowd argues over his identity (Gates, *The
Signifying Monkey* 33-35). The situation in *Tar Baby* is similar in
many respects. From varying angles we see a pageant in which
black and white change meanings, where Brer Rabbit and Brer Fox
change places, and where tar babies seem to turn up everywhere.
Such a world stands in contrast to the world of Conrad, where the
darkness is always out there, never on board. It comes and goes,
but the ship stays on course.

The characters in *Tar Baby* are thus unaware of themselves; in
fact, Morrison suggests that the self is almost unknowable. At the
same time she suggests that these characters fail to see the world
around them. They do not understand each other, but also they do
not understand nature. All of these characters exist in a world that
is implicitly compared to paradise. The moon is always full (43),
the bees have no sting (81), and the morning rain stays in the
mouths of the orchids until noon (81). But much like Lincoln's
Heaven in *Song of Solomon*, this paradise is destroyed by the
whites who have developed it. The opening sentence in chapter one
masterfully understates the situation: "The end of the world, as it
turned out, was nothing more than a collection of magnificent
winter houses on Isle des Chevaliers" (9). But Morrison's point is
clear: Valerian and his neighbors are the destroyers of the world,

a world of which they have no real awareness. "Insulted" and "brokenhearted," with no direction and ultimately no motion, its course altered by man's buildings, the river on Isle de Chevaliers stops, "like a grandmother"(10). The champion daisy trees, a part of the rain forest, know the end of the river means the end of the world. But ironically Valerian names his house "L'Arbe de la Croix" and spends the major part of his time in a greenhouse where he worries about the propagation of plants. He ruins the world's garden (the rain forest), but in its place he builds his own private garden, completely unaware of the destruction he has wrought outside. Valerian's greenhouse is a private world where he can control nature. According to the narrator, "he built the greenhouse as a place of controlled ever-flowering life to greet death in" (63). But just as Valerian's refusal to know keeps him from seeing what he has done to those in his family, so he never learns what he has done to nature. At the end of the novel in near senility, he is still in his greenhouse. Sidney notices the natural world reasserting itself. The bricks that edged the courtyard have been "popping" out of the ground "like they were poked from beneath" (284). The soldier ants have eaten through the speaker wires; the trees have obscured the washhouse. Sidney understands that "this place dislocates everything" (284), but Valerian never does.

Brer Rabbit ultimately escapes Brer Fox by manipulation. He gets Brer Fox to throw him into the briar patch, his natural element. Thus, he blends back into the world that he was made for, born and bred for. Valerian has also manipulated those around him, the servants, the masters, and nature itself. But his briar patch is an artificial one, and the only way for it to blend back into nature is for it to be destroyed as nature reasserts itself. Morrison never tells us whether it is.

Ironically, despite the fact that Son comes into the novel from the sea, he has similar problems blending into the natural world.

Unlike Valerian, he has an understanding of nature; his dramatic effect upon Valerian's plants shows us that. But by the end of the novel, like Valerian, he finds no natural world to blend back into. He has lost the ability to look at the photographs Jadine made in Eloe without thinking of his own people as primitives, people to whom he cannot return. Thus, the choice that Thérèse forces upon him at the end of the novel strikes at the very core of his being. Will he choose the blind horsemen who live close to nature, who represent his past? Or will he choose Jadine, the modern black woman who has left the past behind, who wears a coat made from the skins of ninety baby seals? Just as we never know whether Valerian's greenhouse will be destroyed, so we never know which Son will choose. We can assume, however, that despite his name, he is no less of an orphan now than Jadine and the rest of these characters. Having lost his mother to death, having left his father and the other "primitives" behind for the second time, he is very much like Jadine, Valerian, and Margaret: one who is cut off from the past and has no clear vision of the future. He would like to blend back into nature as Brer Rabbit does, but he has no clear idea where or what the briar patch is.

So in some ways Son is like Ishmael: "another orphan." And it is hard to miss the pointed contrast to *Song of Solomon*. In that novel roots were discovered; here they are destroyed, both literally and figuratively, or we discover that they never existed. The tension in that novel was a matter of words and myths: the reclaiming of language and the retelling, the reappropriation of stories. Here the matter is quite different. The tension is everywhere: in the gulf between black and white, past and present, master and servant, husband and wife, lovers—indeed within the very core of the self. The end of this novel shows us not a man like Milkman, who has come to know himself, but a man who has come to understand that he does not know himself. So it is appropriate that Morrison should use her allusion to the tar baby story to undercut her allusion to "The Secret Sharer." There is a kind of hidden Africanism in the color imagery that Conrad uses, in the assumptions he makes. Morrison's novel shows us that the self is neither black nor white; it is both. Furthermore, its secrets are deeper than the ocean, and they reside in each of us, black and white, perpetually dividing us and bringing us together.

Isle de Chevalier is an edenic realm, very much in the manner that America was to the first settlers. But as the harmony of Eden was lost through a desire for forbidden fruit, so the harmony of Isle de Chevalier was lost through greed. The white settlers destroyed it with their vacation homes and their plush lifestyles. And in the process they uprooted not only the trees of the rain forest but also the human lives that make up the island. In some respects, the same thing happened in America. *Song of Solomon* was the story of one man who found the roots of his past, buried beneath the rubble of history; this novel shows us one man who quite possibly loses his connection to the past. In so doing, he becomes like everyone else on the island: an orphan. Thus, though the white settlers might have destroyed the land, the disease they bring affects all who live there.

In the context of this universal disease, the inscription which begins this novel seems quite appropriate:

> For it hath been declared
> unto me of you, my brethren, by them
> which are of the house of
> Chloe, that there are contentions among you.
> (I Corinthians 1:11)

In writing to the Corinthians, Paul's situation was in some ways like Morrison's as she writes to an American audience. Corinth was a city known for its cosmopolitan population and for its profligacy. The church in Corinth was divided into at least four groups: some proclaimed Paul as their leader; some proclaimed

Christ; others worshipped Christ, still others Apollo (Neil 439). Paul hoped through his letter to bring a divided people together. Morrison seems to have no such hope in her novel. The people to whom she writes are not just divided from one another; they are divided within themselves.

Notes

1. I quote Morrison on this matter:
"I would not be understood to argue that Melville was engaged in some simple and simple-minded black/white didacticism, or that he was satanizing white people. Nothing like that. What I am suggesting is that he was overwhelmed by the philosophical and metaphysical inconsistencies of an extraordinary and unprecedented idea that had its fullest manifestation in his own time in his own country, and that that idea was the successful assertion of whiteness as ideology" (214).

2. Valerian acknowledges that he is named for a Roman emperor, but Morrison leaves it to her readers to discover the particular failings of Valerian's namesake. Publius Licinius Valerianus became emperor in A.D. 253, divided the empire, and was captured in a military disaster by the Persian ruler Shapur I in A.D. 260. He ended his life as a servant who used his back to assist Shapuer in mounting his horse (Payne 275-277). Morrison's point seems fairly clear. Though Valerian may appear to be the master, he actually has less and less control over the world in which he lives. Like his namesake, he is a royal footstool.

SIX

Beloved:

Narratives of the Self

The tension in *Beloved* is in many ways more subtle than the tension in the earlier novels. There is no primer version of reality to begin this novel, nor is there the disparity between a black community, such as the Bottom, and a white community, such as Medallion. There are no allusions to mainstream novels or to the stories or motifs of mainstream novels. Morrison has stated that she attempted in this novel to leave the reader with nothing familiar: "Here I wanted the compelling confusion of being there as they (the characters) are; suddenly, without comfort or succor from the 'author,' with only imagination, intelligence, and necessity available for the journey" ("Unspeakable" 229). Thus, the novel centers around the stories of a number of slaves. But by their very existence, these stories produce a peculiar kind of tension. Most accounts of slavery have been written; these are oral. Most accounts of slavery have focused upon slavery itself; this account contextualizes the slave's experience within his or her subsequent life. Moreover, this account involves a ghost. Importantly, the ghost in *Beloved* is not presented as a shadowy figure, a creature of legend or dreams, but rather as a character who drinks water, has sexual urges, and even has a need for mothering.

This story places constant demands upon the reader. As Trudier Harris has shown, the oral quality of the novel puts the reader into the position of listener (*Fiction and Folklore* 170-171). A listener is more immediate than a reader; the book in the hand is replaced by a presence that directly confronts the audience. Thus, readers of *Beloved* must witness the struggle of each of these characters, hear their stories—not their public, published stories, but their private, oral stories. Further, as Morrison states, her readers must feel "the compelling confusion of being there"; they too must be haunted by the ghost. Thus, the rhetorical strategy that Morrison uses in this novel is quite different from that which she uses in her earlier novels. Those novels present black life within the context of white expectation, but those expectations always have a concrete embodiment: the grade-school primer, Medallion, the *Bildungsroman*, or "The Secret Sharer." In this novel Morrison's main subject is a matter of historical fact—slave narratives, history books. These are the accounts of slavery that her audience has come to expect. Morrison's account differs pointedly from those in its emphasis upon personal lives, told stories, and ghosts. Never within her novel does she clearly allude to these other accounts; nonetheless, by her choice of subjects, they are invoked.

Until recently, the history of slavery came largely from white historians. Moreover, even the slaves who wrote their own personal accounts of slave life initially garnered an audience through the abolitionist movement, which was controlled by whites. Literary critic and historian John Sekora points this out: "Former slaves were wanted..., not for their personal identities as men and women, but for their value as eyewitnesses and victims" (154). He later notes that in the slave narrative, the "meaning, relation, and wholeness of the story are given before the narrative opens... [they are] imposed rather than chosen" (154). The vehicle of this imposition was the white man's letter. Normally presented as a preface or introduction to the narrative, it verified the legitimacy of the document, stating that a black man or woman really did write the text. The narrative was thus a means to an end. The abolitionist movement used the document to argue that if blacks could write, they should not be treated as animals. Moreover, if the document presented the horrors of slavery, these atrocities were associated not with the suffering of that particular slave, but with the horror of the whole institution of slavery. As Raymond Hedin states, "the force of the slave narrative was predicated on the narrator's claim that his or her story was not unique, that it represented countless others as well" (30). In large measure, the point of the narrative was not free expression but rather political maneuvering. And as well-intentioned and vital as that maneuvering might have been, it still did not allow the slave to stand before an audience and explain the particularity of his or her situation. The ex-slave author was often merely a persona for the editor and co-author—the abolitionist.

What is more, the slaves who wrote these narratives were far from representative; they were exceptional in both their determination to learn and their good fortune in getting the opportunity to learn. Frederick Douglass is a good example. Though he essentially taught himself to read without his master's knowledge, there was a stimulus. Mrs. Auld, the master's wife, taught Douglass the alphabet before her husband found out what she was doing. As Douglass puts it, "Mistress, in teaching me the alphabet had given me the inch, no precaution could prevent me from taking the ell" (51).

Morrison's slaves are not so fortunate. Not one of them masters the written language to the extent that Douglass does, yet they still have stories to tell that are vital to their survival as people. But it is the particularity of these stories that Morrison emphasizes. Her slaves are far from typical. Sweet Home under Mr. Garner is decidedly better than most plantations in the vicinity, just as under schoolteacher it is decidedly worse. Moreover, the novel is dedicated to a large group of slaves who never got the chance even to tell their stories, let alone write them. According to Amy Schwartz, Morrison said during her book tour for *Beloved* that the "*Sixty Million/ and more*" on the title page refers to the number of Africans who died on the slave ships (Schwartz B7). In fact, Morrison commented on the figure in a 1989 interview with Bonnie Angelo: "Some historians told me 200 million died. The smallest number I got from anybody was 60 million. There were travel accounts of people who were in the Congo—that's a wide river—saying 'We could not get the boat through the river, it was choked with bodies'"(Taylor-Guthrie 257). Such a dedication emphasizes the importance of those untold stories that were out of the reach of traditional historiography and that were not a part of the slave narrative. Moreover, it empha- sizes the private lives of particular slaves. Those slaves who died before they were ever auctioned off were far from representative of slave experience in this country. They never even saw the soil of the United States. But still their particular experience is important. Thus, there is a tension implied in this novel between literacy and orality, between history as written record, as political document, and history as lived experience. Discussing this novel with interviewer Miriam Horn, Morrison said,

> The slave museums in this country are very upbeat and cute. It's all about pretty quilts that the slaves made and costumes in Williamsburg. And it has all been sort of whitewashed, along with a lot of other things in the history of this country,.... (75)

Beloved is in some respects an attempt to do away with the "whitewashing," to examine the past as it was. One aspect of that past is particular experiences so entirely lost to us now that we may only imagine them.

Hence there is a central paradox in the novel. Though the novel is not history in the true sense of the word, it does attempt to acquaint us with the reality of the lives that mainstream historians did not always portray. Using the voices of the slaves who did not write a narrative, Morrison catalogues the dehumanizing treatment to which they were exposed, detailing punishments and executions in the manner of the slave narrative: the burning of Sixo, Paul D's wearing of the bit, the milking and beating of Sethe. Still, this novel is not a slave narrative. It does not purport to be factual, nor does it present the brutality of the slave master for any clear, immediate political end. These incidents are events in particular lives, and Morrison consistently contextualizes them within these lives.

The main focus of the novel is the relationship between Paul D and Sethe. It is in that context that we learn about the past. *Beloved* begins and ends with Paul D and Sethe. Early in the novel, they make love. The last chapter begins with a folk song about love. Paul D returns to Sethe at the end of the novel because he recognizes his need for her. But Paul D and Sethe can only come to one another through the reality of their past. For them love can exist only in the context of their history. Thus, throughout this novel, personal lives and history stand in conflict. This conflict becomes another source of tension.

Repeatedly in this novel, freedom is linked to the ability to love. For Paul D it is easier to love inanimate nature than it is to love human beings. Lying in bed with Sethe, he is revolted by the clump of scars on her back. He thinks that though Sethe called them a "a chokecherry tree," they are nothing like a real tree "because trees are inviting" (21). He then remembers a tree he sat under at Sweet Home, a tree he named "Brother." Paul D's reasoning makes sense only in the context of his experiences. He has learned that love is "risky": "The best thing, he knew, was to love just a little bit; everything, just a little bit, so when they broke its back, or shoved it in a croaker sack, well, maybe you'd have a little left over for the next one" (45). The same applies to Sethe; she too links freedom to the ability to love. When she arrives in Cincinnati after escaping slavery, she is struck by her sudden freedom to love: "there wasn't nobody in the world I couldn't love if I wanted to" (162). Paul D understands this statement and remembers again "loving small": "Grass blades, salamanders, spiders, woodpeckers, beetles, a kingdom of ants. Anything bigger wouldn't do" (162). Ella, a minor character, looks at Sethe's baby and says "If you ask me I'd say, 'Don't love nothing'" (92). Her statement suggests that love of any sort is not worth the risk.

In such a context, Sethe's act of love for her children is an expression of freedom. She takes the risk and chooses to love them, and when they are threatened, she chooses to act upon her love. According to Cynthia Wolff, even a married white woman had no legal claim to her children in nineteenth-century America. For a slave mother, the situation was much worse: only her owner had legal claim to her progeny (Wolff 417-418). So Sethe's bold expression of love contradicts all the laws of nineteenth-century America. But ironically, the actions that express that love are in themselves savage. Thus, once again we come to a paradox in the novel. Sethe's act emphasizes the perverse nature of slavery: a mother must kill her children to protect them. Sethe can choose not to love, or she can choose to kill what she loves to protect it. Either choice begets a loss of some part of the self.

Paul D can understand Sethe's need for the freedom to love, but he cannot understand her allowing herself to love so completely, nor can he understand what her love for her children causes her to do. As he says to her after she tries to explain her actions to him, "'Your love is too thick'" (164). Then, after making such a statement, he implies that Sethe acted the part of an animal: "'You got two feet, Sethe, not four'" (165). Paul D is suggesting that despite the horror of the circumstances, there are limits to what any human being should do. But Sethe makes it quite clear that in her eyes she has done the only thing that she possibly can do. In

Sethe's words, "'Thin love ain't love at all'" (165). According to Bernard Bell, Morrison often says in her lectures, "'What is curious to me,'... 'is that bestial treatment of human beings never produces a race of beasts'" (272). In seeking to love one another, to love children, these characters seek to recover their humanity, to avoid becoming "a race of beasts." Thus, Paul D's comments present us with the paradox at the center of this novel: in protecting Beloved by killing her, Sethe risks losing her own humanity. In exploring such a situation, Morrison is setting forth a kind of history that was never a part of traditional histories of slavery. She is suggesting that the slave was not just deprived of rights or even life itself. He or she was deprived of the freedom to be human.

Despite its importance, the slave narrative could not fully address this issue. As Henry Louis Gates points out, the abolition movement proved black humanity by demonstrating black facility with language: if a black man or woman could write, then he or she shared white humanity and should not be treated as an animal. As a consequence, there was always a correlation between literacy and freedom. Black writers wrote and were encouraged to write to counter racist allegations that "because blacks had no written traditions they were bearers of an inferior culture" (*Figures* 25). Writers of slave narratives use language to suggest to their readers that readers and writers share common humanity. Thus, Douglass may argue with his reader that slavery is brutal; he may use his own victimization to prove such a point. But always he stands before the reader fully humanized, communicating in proper English. He appeals to reason. The white reader identifies with him and sympathizes with him. Even when Douglass reveals his suffering, it is filtered through the language of the abolitionist narrative: "I was sometimes prompted to take my life, and that of Covey, but was prevented by a combination of hope and fear. My sufferings on this plantation seem now like a dream rather than a stern reality" (74).

Douglass's contribution to our knowledge of slavery, to American literature is important. As John Sekora points out, Douglass is able to speak with individuality despite the constraints of the form in which he writes (156). But the genre in which he writes is quite different from the genre in which Morrison writes. The *Narrative* shows us the outside of a character, the public self; Morrison's novel shows us the inside, the private self. Her main character does not recover from slavery as Douglass seems to within the *Narrative*. She commits an act that is by nature inhuman and lives a shattered life, not communicating with those around her. Douglass goes on to become an ardent spokesperson for his race. The reader and Paul D must struggle to understand what Sethe has done. Throughout the novel there is a kind of tension that Paul D implies in his accusation: Sethe's love is "too thick" and as a result she has acted as an animal would. We are seeing the jagged ends of the slave experience, not just the long-sought freedom, but the nightmare of trying to live freely again.

The other slaves in the novel are in some respects similar to Sethe. Though they do not commit brutal acts to protect their children, each has a moment in which his or her basic humanity is in question. Morrison's narrator tells of Baby Suggs' ride to freedom with Mr. Garner:

> But suddenly she saw her hands and thought with a clarity as simple as it was dazzling, "These my hands." Next she felt a knocking in her chest and discovered something new: her own heartbeat. Had it been there all along? This pounding thing? (141).

Baby Suggs then expresses these things to Mr. Garner, who laughs without comprehending the significance of what she says to him. Though Baby Suggs never saw but one of her seven children grow up, ultimately she knows more about each of them than she knows about herself, "having never had the map to discover what she was like" (140). Later, when Mr. Garner asks her about her name, Baby

Suggs responds with these words: "'Nothing.... I don't call myself nothing'" (142). A woman who does not own hands or heart would hardly be expected to have a name.

Paul D's story has a similar focal point. Paul D's past is represented by the rusted-shut tobacco can which he carries in his breast pocket. The narrator tells us that it contains all of Paul D's past: "Alfred, Georgia, Sixo, schoolteacher, Halle, his brothers, Sethe, Mister, the taste of iron, the sight of butter, the smell of hickory, notebook paper" (113). It is so firmly closed that "nothing in this world could pry it open" (113). But because of the relationship that he develops with Sethe, Paul D tells her stories he has never told. He opens the can. Telling her the story of the punishment he received from schoolteacher, his focus is similar to that of Baby Suggs: the emptiness of being a slave. While being punished with "the bit," he sees Mister, a rooster whom he pulled from a half-cracked egg shell and watched grow into the most feared bird in the barnyard. It is the contrast between his own state and Mister's that causes him to see himself clearly as a slave:

> "Mister, he looked so...free. Better than me. Stronger, tougher,....
> Mister was allowed to be and stay what he was. But I wasn't allowed
> to be and stay what I was. Even if you cooked him you'd be cooking
> a rooster named Mister. But wasn't no way I'd ever be Paul D again,
> living or dead." (72)

When he finishes telling this story, the narrator states that Paul D fears Sethe will learn the full truth: "that there was no red heart bright as Mister's comb beating in him" (73). Both of these stories emphasize what Sethe's story does: the loss of humanity that slavery entails. Like Sethe, Paul D and Baby Suggs are divided selves. They do not know the intimate details of themselves—their names, their hands, their hearts, their past. Slavery has stolen vital parts of themselves.

Significantly, the stories of Baby Suggs and Paul D unravel slowly, told in stolen moments by the characters to each other, or told by the narrator in the context of conversations among characters. These stories are oral and personal. They echo the story of Sethe, the focal point of the novel. What is more, they stand in contrast to the slave narrative, a public document which was used for a public cause: the fight against slavery. They also stand in contrast to the history book, another public document, incapable of rendering private experience. The narrator emphasizes the private nature of these stories when she states at the end of the novel, "this is not a story to pass on" (275). Public stories are meant to be passed on; this one is private. What is more, this statement sets up another contrast in the novel: the contrast between Sethe's told story of the killing of Beloved and Stamp Paid's newspaper clipping. Sethe's story is oral; the newspaper account is written. Sethe's story is private; the newspaper account is public. The newspaper account is a historical document; Sethe's account reflects her experience, her memory. These contrasts demonstrate to us again the subversive nature of Morrison's work. Bakhtin says that "every language in the novel is a point of view, a socio-ideological conceptual system of real social groups and their embodied system" (*Dialogic* 411). Morrison thus emphasizes the contrast between the official version of slave history and the private lives of slaves by juxtaposing Sethe's language with the newspaper account, an account we never hear, though we clearly feel its presence.

Stamp Paid reluctantly shows Paul D the clipping from the newspaper concerning Sethe's crime. Even so, the very fact that he has kept the clipping is significant. Unlike Paul D, Stamp Paid can read. What is more, Paul D's reaction to the clipping is sudden and intense: he shakes his head "no." The narrator makes clear that Paul D's reaction is not unusual, for to anyone of black skin, literate or illiterate, slave stories in the newspaper had an unmistakable meaning:

> A whip of fear broke through the heart chambers as soon as you saw a Negro's face in a paper since the face was not there because the person had a healthy baby.... It would have to be something out of the ordinary—something white people would find interesting, truly different, worth a few minutes of teeth sucking if not gasps. (156)

Morrison is returning to the issue of the ownership of words, one of the central concerns of *Song of Solomon*. The newspaper is the product of white society. Nonetheless, Stamp Paid seems to acknowledge this system, to know that those definitions matter: "From the solemn air with which Stamp had unfolded the paper, the tenderness in the old man's fingers as he stroked its creases and flattened it out, first on his knees, then on the split top of the piling, Paul D knew that it ought to mess him up" (154). Moreover, Stamp Paid refuses to tell Paul D the story. In fact, the narrator emphasizes that the oral version of the story is in Stamp's mind, repeating, "So Stamp Paid did not tell him...." (157). Rather, he reads Paul D the story from the newspaper: "Instead he took a breath and leaned toward the mouth that was not hers and slowly read out the words Paul D couldn't" (158). As Stamp Paid shows him the clipping, Paul D looks at the picture of Sethe in the newspaper clipping and says, "That aint her mouth" (154). He does not recognize Sethe as she appears in the newspaper. But ironically, when Sethe tells him the story, he still fails to understand what she has done because her words do not have any more power to explain her actions than the white newspaper. As the narrator implies, it is a private story.

Sethe's words to Paul D are almost without emotion: "'I stopped him,'.... 'I took and put my babies where they'd be safe'" (164). But as she remembers the event, her thinking is nearly wordless: "And if she thought anything it was No. No. Nono.

Nonono. Simple. She just flew" (163). Sethe cannot explain her actions in words because the core of Sethe's story is beyond language. Still, it is important that Sethe tells what she can of her story.

I began this chapter with Trudier Harris' observation that a primary difference between orality and literacy is the immediacy of the audience in the first and the remoteness of it in the latter (*Fiction and Folklore* 170-171). Such an observation helps us with this scene. The newspaper clipping imposes a definition upon Sethe's actions. We may disagree with that definition, but the author of it is beyond our reach. Moreover, that definition carries with it the sanction of mainstream society; it is, to use Bakhtin's phrase, "a socio-ideological conceptual system" (*Dialogic* 411). But Sethe's story is quite different. As Harris argues, the oral quality of her story forces Paul D to question her, and it forces the reader to question her. In fact, in some respects, Paul D is a foil for the reader, for they both must work to understand what Sethe has done. Morrison has thus presented three orders of experience. Paul D hears the story as it is presented in the newspaper. He also hears Sethe's attempt to explain what she did. He cannot accept or understand either one of these versions of the story. But there is one final version of the story: the private version that Sethe remembers. This story is a series of memories, wordless, almost beyond thought itself: "And if she thought anything it was No. No. NoNo" (163). This wordlessness shows us the ultimate distinction between private narratives and public narratives. Some experiences cannot be put into words; they can only be felt. Sethe's thoughts take us to that realm. They show us that the ultimate pain of slavery is beyond slave narratives and history books, beyond language itself. Consequently, the modern reader will never fully understand Sethe's pain or her act.

The reader's role in this novel is still vitally important. The tension between orality and literacy is the center of this novel.

Beloved exists in written form, but in some respects, by insisting that each slave tell his or her story, Morrison forces her reader to respond to the book as an oral form, to become involved in the telling. Moreover, as Trudier Harris observes, by presenting her readers with such unresolved moral issues, Morrison insists upon her readers' involvement (*Fiction and Folklore* 170-171). But the moral issues do not end with Sethe; ultimately Morrison involves the reader in more immediate moral issues. She begins this process on the title page with the inscription which comes from Romans:

I will call them my people,
which were not my people;
and her beloved,
which was not beloved.
Romans 9:2

Applying this quotation to the novel forces the reader to become involved in its meaning, not just in the sense of making the reader an interpreter, but also in the sense of forcing him or her into the presence of the characters. Earlier I quoted Morrison's statement that she intended for the reader to have no "comfort or succor" in this novel. This epigram is an expression of that intent, for it leaves the reader with no escape from the history this book presents. Each reader is the "I" in the quotation; each character thus becomes "my people."

Looking at the inscriptions in this light enlarges the ambiguities of the novel, for not only must readers ponder the paradox of Sethe's act, but also they must accept the reality of what school- teacher and his understudies did. The words "my people" in the inscription imply that every American reader has a past that is a part of this novel. There is no escape for anyone in the audience. Black readers must accept the suffering that was a part of their past, and white readers must accept the brutality that was a part of their past. What is more, in some respects, the reader becomes very much like Sethe. He or she is a person who lives in a haunted house. In order for the house guests to leave, they must be faced, talked to, called "beloved": as the passage from Romans says, *"I will call...her beloved,/ which was not beloved."* Thus, this novel forces readers to confront slavery in a way that history books and slave narratives cannot. It is for that reason that the ghost in the story is so important.

As the embodiment of the past, the ghost functions again and again to emphasize the inescapable reality of history.[1] The first lines of the novel present the ghost not as something that might be or that is perceived by some of the characters, but as something that is: "124 was spiteful. Full of baby's venom. The women in the house knew and so did the children" (3). The presence of the ghost is made concrete in the same chapter when Paul D wrestles with it, saying "'You want to fight, come on'" (18). This ghost is no shadowy presence; it is a daily part of the household, a daily threat to living. So it is with the past.

Still curiously, when the ghost is most concrete, fully embodied, the adults fail to recognize her. Denver knows that Beloved comes from "over there" (75); she even asks her about it. But Sethe does not realize that she recognizes Beloved until early in Part Two of the novel. Significantly, Paul D has just left because of what he has learned about Sethe. Sethe's response to Paul D's leaving is to move inward: "Whatever is going on outside my door ain't for me" (183). It is in this context that she understands "the click" that came much earlier. "The click" is the knowledge that Denver has from the first: that Beloved is the child Sethe murdered. Thus, it is in isolation that Sethe comes to know the ghost fully, and it is in isolation that the ghost comes to prey upon Sethe. But Morrison once again presents the reader with a paradox. Sethe's confrontation with the ghost is ultimately a private matter; it is only in isolation that she can recognize it. Hers is a private story. But to be rid of it, she must have the help of the community. It is the women Denver brings who find the "sound that broke the back of words," ultimately making Sethe tremble "like the baptized in its wash" (261). They are the ones who save Sethe from the ghost who haunts her every move and threatens her very life.

So, despite the personal nature of these stories, this novel has a larger dimension. Paul, the writer of the inscription with which the novel begins, placed himself in a very public arena. In Romans, he wrote to a church divided by racial prejudice. He sought to settle ethnic squabbles in which Gentile and Jew saw each other as villains, saw each other as lacking basic humanity in the eyes of God. Paul's mission was to bring these people together, to enable them to recognize within themselves and within each other the same human and divine being.[1] And perhaps that is the final import of the inscription: to suggest that each reader must accept not only his past, her past, but also those around him or her. Thus, this novel addresses a major element of American life. The ghost belongs to all of us, and we must deal with it alone and as a society. Beloved is not just the child that Sethe murdered; she is the past that each of us ignores, the "*sixty million and more*" who, according to Morrison, died on slave ships. But she is more: she is the enslaver and the enslaved that haunts the house of each American, black and white. And thus, at the end of the novel though the ghost is vanquished, Morrison makes clear that she has not disappeared. Though the ghost haunted Sethe, Morrison leaves no doubt that she belongs to all of us. And like Sethe, we know her, even if we do not acknowledge her: "Everybody knew what she was called, but nobody anywhere knew her name. Disremembered and unaccounted for, she cannot be lost because no one is looking for her, and even if they were, how can they call her if they don't know her name?" (274). This novel allows us to know the name and to know the presence. The opening inscription demands that we call her name.

Morrison has said that she wrote *Beloved* because she was haunted by the story of Margaret Garner, the slave from Cincinnati who murdered a child to save it from the slave master (Wolff 417).[3] Much like Sethe, she had a ghost to deal with. And in the process of escaping that ghost, she makes each of us aware of a past that often is unacknowledged. But once again, she places that past in the context of American experience, specifically addressing and in some respects undermining a traditional American understanding of history, of slavery, of personal responsibility. With a ghost that is inescapable, she reminds us once again of the brutal past that slumbers in the collective memory of our national consciousness. It is only through acknowledging the past that each of us can escape the ghost. It is only through knowing each other that we, like Sethe, can escape being devoured by what we acknowledge.

Notes

1. Carol Schmudde makes a similar point in her article "The Haunting of 124": "But Beloved may be unique in using the ghost story to shock its readers into locating the source of horror not in mysteries beyond this world but rather in the repressed and unclaimed realities of the factual, historical past" (415).

2. In his recent article, "Giving Blood to the Scraps: Haints, History, and Hosea in *Beloved*," Robert Broad interprets this inscription quite differently from the way in which I do. He points out Paul's allusion to Hosea, a Jewish prophet, interpreting Morrison's use of the passage as a commentary on the reappropriation of language. In Broad's reading Paul becomes not the one who seeks racial unity but the one who ignores ethnic roots (190-196).

3. For an excellent account of the historical figure whom Morrison uses as a model for Sethe, see the article by Cynthia Griffin Wolff, "'Margaret Garner': a Cincinnati Story," *The Massachusetts Review* 32 (Fall 1991): 417-440.

SEVEN

Jazz:

Seeking the Name of the Sound

Jazz is the first of Morrison's novels that has focused exclusively upon romantic love. In *Beloved* and *Tar Baby* romance is the central concern of the main characters. But other issues command the reader's attention in these novels. In *Tar Baby* the main issue is always Jadine's lack of a past and Son's rootedness, the conflict of past and present in the characters and their relationships. In *Beloved*, the love between Paul D and Sethe is consistently thwarted by their slave past, a matter so important that the reader notices it as much as he or she notices the romance between Paul D and Sethe. But in *Jazz* the focus seems exclusively to be love. The first paragraph emphasizes its importance: "He fell for an eighteen-year-old girl with one of those deepdown, spooky loves that made him so sad and happy he shot her just to keep the feeling going" (3).

Reviewers have noticed the romantic relationships at the center of *Jazz*, and for several of them the romance Morrison presents is not convincing. Edna O'Brien in *The New York Times Book Review* complains that "the emotional nexus" is missing from this novel (30). Paul Gray of *Time* magazine complains that Morrison "never convincingly accounts for the horror that Joe and Violet feel compelled to wreak" (70). But such complaints fail to recognize the importance of the title. This is a novel written about the kind of love we find in blues or jazz songs. In such songs desire and violence are an expected part of the setting. Moreover, they are often intermingled. Furthermore, the listener is never given any more than the bare minimum number of details. Morrison thus reveals the entire plot on the first page of the novel. Also, as many critics have observed, music is quite literally everywhere in this novel: in the air, in the characters' minds, in the narrator's mind.[1] Thus, though love may be Morrison's central focus, music becomes the central component of her rhetorical strategy. It enables her to use the indefinable quality of black music to undercut certainty, tradition, hegemony itself. To understand this strategy, we must once again turn to Bakhtin.

In discussing Rabelais, Bakhtin observes that the spirit of parody "was intensified to the point where it became a parody of the very act of conceptualizing anything in language" (*Dialogic* 309). In a similar vein, Bakhtin states in *Rabelais and His World* that "The last word of the epoch, sincerely and seriously asserted, was not Rabelais's last word" (453). Rabelais's last word could only be found "in the popular-festive elemental imagery." Here Rabelais leaves "a loophole that opens on the distant future and that lends an aspect of ridicule to the relative progressiveness and relative truth accessible to the present or to the immediate future" (454). To some extent Morrison uses jazz (a musical idiom from popular culture) just as Bakhtin asserts that Rabelais used "popular-festive elemental imagery." For her the very indefinable quality of jazz becomes the essence of her characters, indeed of humanity in general. It enables her to undercut the clearly defined and rigidly conceptualized world of tradition. It becomes the ultimate way of saying, to borrow Bakhtin's phrase, that there is "no last word."

Throughout *Jazz* the characters are linked to music. Joe Trace and his elusive mother, Wild, have an untraceable lineage.

Similarly, the origins and development of jazz are shrouded in mystery. According to *The Oxford English Dictionary*, the word jazz has no known origin. Furthermore, according to musicologists, establishing and tracing the lineage of jazz as a musical idiom is almost impossible (Schuller 4). Moreover, even defining the term is largely a matter of conjecture. Barry Ulanov says at the beginning of *A History of Jazz in America* that "No common definition of this music has been reached" (3). The term itself has numerous associations that have little to do with music. According to *The Oxford English Dictionary*, the term can mean "to speed or liven *up*." It can also mean to have sexual intercourse. At least one theory ties its origin to the French term *jaser*, which means "to pep up, to exhilarate" (Ulanov 6).

Morrison's novel reflects a number of these shades of meaning. It focuses on characters who are in many respects orphans. Like jazz, their origins are shrouded in mystery. Joe Trace seeks his alleged mother, Wild, in the forest. He never finds her, and he never knows for sure that she is his mother. At the end of the novel, he wonders whether in searching for Dorcas he is actually still seeking his mother. Violet is little different. Her father is an evasive figure who periodically appears bearing gifts and then quietly vanishes. Her mother, Rose Dear, commits suicide by jumping in a well. Dorcas is much like Joe and Violet in this regard. Her parents are killed in the East Saint Louis race riots, and she is raised by the over-protective, repressive Alice Manfred. A large portion of the novel concerns Golden Gray and his search for his black father. Even Felice, who is Dorcas's friend, and after her death a frequent visitor at the Trace home, comes to the Traces initially looking for the ring her mother gave her. Separated from both of her parents, she sees the ring as a concrete embodiment of her mother's love. Thus, all of these characters have a parent whom they seek and often do not find. Like that of jazz itself, their lineage is indefinite, uncertain. Like it, they are rootless denizens of an urban world.

In such an environment the characters in *Jazz* directly confront "their stronger, riskier selves"(33), often sexually. This characteristic ties them to jazz. Morrison's narrator describes carefully the nature of urban life. If jazz means to exhilarate, to pep up, then it is very much like the urban world of which Joe and Violet become a part: "There is no air in the City but there is breath, and every morning it races through him ["a man"] like laughing gas brightening his eyes, his talk, and his expectations" (34). If jazz implies sex, then the relationship between Joe and Dorcas is a kind of jazz. When Joe describes to Malvonne the emptiness of his relationship with Violet, sexuality and verve are tied to one another: "'She don't talk anymore, and I aint allowed near her. Any other man be running around, stepping out every night, you know that. I aint like that. I aint.'" The narrator then exposes the character's rationalization: "Of course, he wasn't, but he did it anyway" (49). A kind of jazz is missing from his life; sex with Dorcas supplies it. So in a sense, he is "like that."

Like Joe, all of the other characters seek something to enliven them; often, they seek something indefinable. Violet steals a baby, and though she returns it within minutes, years later she remembers "the light...that had skipped through her veins" (22). Despite the dull, uneventfulness of Malvonne's life, within herself she creates a kind of fantasy world: "When she was not making her office building sparkle, she was melding the print stories with her keen observation of people around her" (41). She even vicariously enters other lives when she reads and acts upon the bag of unmailed letters that her son Sweetness steals. Even Alice Manfred, who consciously resists the power of the "dirty, get-on-down music the women sang" because "it made you do unwise, disorderly things," still feels its charm (58): "Alice carried that gathering rope with her always after that day on Fifth Avenue, and found it reliably secure and tight—most of the time. Except when the men sat on windowsills fingering horns" (58). The world Morrison creates here is alive with "jazz." Whether through sex or merely involvement in the lives of others, every character seeks exhilaration. Since most of them are orphans, we have a poignant picture of urban life: orphaned souls all seeking something to enliven, to complete themselves.

The same could be said of the jazz musician: he too seeks something elusive and indefinable. Barry Ulanov quotes various musicians as they try to define "swing," which, according to Ulanov, is the 1935 term for jazz. Jess Stacy calls it "'Syncopated syncopation.'" Louis Armstrong calls it "'My idea of how a tune should go.'" Ella Fitzgerald says "'Why, er—swing is—well, you sort of feel—uh—uh—I don't know—you just swing.'" Chuck Webb probably provides the most innovative definition: "'Its like lovin' a gal, and havin' a fight, and then seein' her again.'" The common thread in all of these definitions is expressed by Glenn Miller: he says that swing is "'something that you have to feel'" (5). Moreover, to the musician jazz is something he or she seeks. As Ulanov says, "To get the elusive beat, a jazzman will do anything. Without it, he cannot do anything" (6). The implication here is that the musician is constantly seeking something that he finds for only a moment in his music, something that is never caught but always to be caught. Since all of the characters in *Jazz* seek something that they cannot find, they clearly have affinity with the jazz musician. We see a clear example of this connection in Joe Trace's search for Wild.

At various points in his search for his elusive mother, he feels that he is near her. He sees things that are associated with her—red winged blackbirds, ruined honeycombs—but never does he see her. Still, he associates her with music. While in the woods, he hears what he thinks is "the music of the world" (176). Then he hears in addition to this "The scrap of song...from a woman's throat"

(177). He senses his mother, but he never sees her. Very quickly he loses even the song. Morrison makes clear that his relationship with Dorcas and his search for his mother are part of the same impulse. As he seeks the unfaithful Dorcas with his gun, he remembers the search for his mother. By the end of chapter seven, the two searches have become one. The closing question thus becomes an ominous one: "But where is *she*? (184). Indeed, the narrator expresses at the end of the novel her own surprise: "All the while he was running through the streets in bad weather I thought he was looking for her [Dorcas], not Wild's chamber of gold" (221). Joe himself tells Felice that he killed Dorcas because he did not know how to love her. When she asks him if he has learned how, he says, "'No. Do you, Felice?'" (213). Like jazz, love is elusive and enlivening. For Joe Trace it is something that he seeks but never finds. Golden Gray's search is essentially the same. He seeks first his father, then the same indefinable character whom Joe seeks: Wild, a character whose very name suggests mystery and passion.

Just as Joe seeks his missing mother throughout the novel (even in his search for Dorcas), so Violet's love for Joe is a way of confronting the loss of a mother. When their relationship begins, the narrator states, "Never again would she wake struggling against the pull of a narrow well. Or watch first light with the sadness left over from finding Rose Dear [Violet's mother] in the morning twisted into water much too small" (104). But later in life, Violet longs to be a mother. In part, it is the nature of city life that keeps her from having children. Her miscarriages are "inconveniences," not losses, because "citylife would be so much better without them [children]" (107). Yet by the age of forty, Violet is longing after children: "staring at infants, hesitating in front of toys displayed at Christmas" (107). And just as Joe in seeking Dorcas is also seeking his mother, so Violet allows Dorcas (or at least her picture) to become a substitute for her child: "Was she [Dorcas] the woman who took the man, or the daughter who fled her womb?" (109). Thus, for Violet as well as for Joe, Dorcas becomes a symbol for the elusive love she seeks. The mingling of desire in these relationships is important. Love of mother for child, child for mother, lover for lover—all are like "the beat" that the jazz musician seeks when he plays, like Golden Gray's search first for his father and later for Wild. What is more, in the context of urban life, the characters do unusual things because of their desire.

Joe shoots Dorcas; Violet carves her corpse. Violet sits in the street and later steals a baby. As bizarre as these acts are, they once again take us back to the nature of jazz. In blues, one important component of jazz, desire and violence are often intertwined.[2] What is more, blues presents to the hearer a constant sense of incompleteness. Its roots are in the spiritual, but as Ulanov argues, the blues shifts the focus of the spiritual from God and heaven to "man's devilish life on earth" (26). Such a life is exactly the focus of Morrison's novel.

Robert Johnson, the famed Mississippi blues songwriter of the twenties and thirties, experienced the life so often chronicled in blues songs. He died in his early thirties, either poisoned by a woman or stabbed by her jealous husband. In his piece "Me and the Devil Blues" desire and violence are clearly related. The narrator of the song wakes up early in the morning to the sound of Satan knocking upon his door. He and the devil leave, seeking the narrator's girlfriend. He plans to beat her until he finds satisfaction (Tirro 129). Even more common are blues songs which explore unfulfilled longings. A famous example is "What did I do to be so Black and Blue." Though Louis Armstrong's version of the song is best known, Ethel Waters also recorded the song. In her version, she makes the listener poignantly aware of the nature of loneliness, describing a cold, empty bed with hard springs, asking why she was born black and blue (Tirro 143). In other passages in the song, loneliness is the result of being black: the narrator's sin becomes skin color (Tirro 143). Through the vehicle of the song, the blues singer makes his or her private longing, in some cases his very blackness, into something that all people share. As Ulanov argues, "there are fear and sorrow in the laments of Bessie Smith or Ma Rainey, and passion as well—but all laughed or shouted away" (32). Thus, all of these searches for the elusive, for the indefinable express the incompleteness these characters feel, an incompleteness evident in blues. In Morrison's novel, this incompleteness is sometimes associated with white society's discrimination against people of color; other times it is existential.

Joe's affair with Dorcas is not attributable to white culture, nor is Joe's estrangement from his alleged mother. Violet's longing for children is also not a direct product of white culture. But other longings in the novel are brought about by white culture. Violet's loss of Rose Dear, her mother, is the result of Rose Dear's persecution by whites, just as the deaths of Dorcas's parents are in some respects the result of conflict between white and black culture. Golden Gray's identity is clearly shaped by the fact that his father is black and his mother is white. So in some respects the urban lives we see here are very clearly defined by the white world that encompasses them, that has shaped their backgrounds. But Morrison's focus in the novel is on what these characters do in the context of the present: how they deal with loss and estrangement, not how they suffered it. The indefinable, unfulfilled longing at the center of each character in the novel is not just the product of white oppression; it is existential. But still, since longings are at the center of the novel, Morrison's focus is very similar to that of a blues song. Thus, jazz becomes for Morrison a broad vehicle of expression, a universal language of loss and hunger, of desire and doubt, of that indefinable sense of incompleteness.

Repeatedly, the narrator refers to music, the major metaphor of the novel. As Joe sets out to find Dorcas, gun in hand, he dismisses the evil in his thoughts because "I wasn't sure that the sooty music the blind twins were playing wasn't the cause" (132). Later he knows that as he leaves the beauty parlor the women there will gossip about him while they "pat on to that sooty music" (133). In the City, music is as palpable as air, and desire and longing are always part of it: "A colored man floats down out of the sky blowing a saxophone and below him, in the space between two buildings, a girl talks earnestly to a man in a straw hat" (8). Alice Manfred notices the change in the music: "Songs that used to start in the head and fill the heart had dropped on down, down to places below the sash and the buckled belts. Lower and lower, until the music was so lowdown you had to shut your windows..." (56). Joe's very life is described as an expression of desire, and once again the metaphor is music: "It [the track of desire] pulls him like a needle through the groove of a Bluebird record. Round and round about the town (120).[3] As Alice Manfred seems to know, the music has power: "It made you do unwise disorderly things. Just hearing it was like violating the law" (58). In every one of these examples the narrator (or character) is drawing a connection between music and life, rhythm and behavior. Thus, Morrison's emphasis on music enables her to focus on longings that are inescapably human. Alice Manfred's description of music that moves from head to heart to body emphasizes how all-inclusive the music is.

Morrison herself has commented on the all-inclusive nature of jazz: "'After the First World War, black people began to literally color—if I can use that word—the culture of the country,'.... 'And jazz was a big part of that'" (Turbide 51). Morrison's statement accords with what many musicologists have observed. Gunther Schuller states in *Early Jazz* that "jazz represents a transplanted continuation of indigenous African musical traditions" (6). Furthermore, a number of the African qualities of jazz are important when we view them in the context of the novel. Both

African native music and jazz grow out of what Schuller calls "a total vision of life" (4). Music is not a separate domain in African culture as it is in European culture; it is "conditioned by the same stimuli that animate not only African philosophy and religion, but the entire social structure" (4). The practical result of such a point of view is that everything is "rhythmized" (5). In short, there is no part of daily life that is not a part of the rhythm of jazz.

The melodic basis of the "riff" in jazz and of blues in general has a direct source in the tendency of African musicians to center their melodies around a central tone (49). There is also the matter of improvisation. For most casual listeners, this term conjures up the idea of a musician who simply plays what he feels. In actuality, the improvisational quality of jazz is similar to the improvisational quality of African music. It grows out of organizational patterns that can be traced back to call and response singing and the use of a chorus in African music (59). Thus, in Schuller's words, "within the loose framework of European tradition, the American Negro was able to preserve a significant nucleus of his African heritage. And it is that nucleus that has made jazz the uniquely captivating language that it is" (62).

When we look at Morrison's novel in the context of Schuller's comments, we see how important music is to the novel. Jazz incorporates the African musicians' tendency to center their melodies around repetitions. Morrison's novel does the same: she shows us desire in varying guises, always indefinable. Joe's desire is a mixture of a longing for a mother and a longing for sex and love. Violet's desire is also for a mother, but, in addition, for a lover, and then later for a child and finally for the face of Dorcas, her husband's lover and the daughter she never had. The other characters are similar. Dorcas is initially drawn to Joe. He fills the emptiness that is left when her parents died; later, she is drawn to Acton, the man whom she is with when Joe shoots her. Even Alice Manfred, who has consciously shut the door on her desires, remembers the rotting teeth of her former lover when Violet asks her "'Wouldn't you? Wouldn't you fight for your man?'" (85). No one is free of desire, not even those who run from it, not even the unidentified narrator of the novel. At the end of the novel, she confesses, "*I have loved only you, surrendered my whole self reckless to you and nobody else*" (229). Is this the narrator speaking to the reader ("*your fingers on and on, lifting, turning*" [229])? Is she saying that she desires the reader? Or is this the narrator expressing her longing to someone whom she loves? At the beginning of the last chapter in the novel, the narrator asks, "What, I wonder, what would I be without a few brilliant spots of blood to ponder? Without aching words that set, then miss, the mark?" (219). She implies here that the very act of writing itself is an expression of desire. Comparable to the jazz musician, who tries endlessly to find the elusive beat, so the narrator sets the "mark" with her words and misses it. In each of these characters and situations Morrison is focusing upon the indefinable nature of desire and thus giving her reader variations upon the tone with which she began.

This novel is also consciously improvisational. Many of the chapters begin in what seems to be mid-sentence. For example, chapter one starts with "Sth, I know that woman" (3). Chapter two begins with "Or used to be" (27). Chapter three begins with "Like that day in July, almost nine years back, when the beautiful men were cold" (53). The last chapter opens with a single word, "Pain" (219). Even chapters which begin with complete sentences often contain pronouns or coordinating conjunctions which suggest the connectedness of all in the novel. Chapter five starts with this sentence: "And when spring comes to the City people notice one another in the road; notice the strangers with whom they share aisles and tables and the space where intimate garments are laundered" (117). Chapter seven begins with "A thing like that could harm you" (165). Such openings are oral; they bestow upon the reader the immediacy and familiarity of a listener, a member of the community who knows these characters. But more than that, such a device also reminds us of the jazz musician's tendency to use riffs, variations improvised around the same note. All the sections of the novel are connected because they all concern desire. But they are all separate because the narrator is viewing a different character or the same character from a different angle.

It is also important that the narrator tells the reader that she is improvising the story. This is particularly apparent in chapter six. She begins with a portrait of herself: "Risky, I'd say, trying to figure out anybody's state of mind. But worth the trouble if you're like me—curious, inventive and well informed" (137). Later in the chapter we get a glimpse of her relationship to the characters in the novel. She says of Golden Gray, "I like to think of him that way" (150). Still later, she says, "What was I thinking of? How could I have imagined him so poorly?" (160). This whole conjectural narrative quality is underscored by the narrator's confession in the last chapter that she has failed to portray the characters accurately: "So I missed it altogether" (220). It is clear from such a statement that the narrator is improvising, making the story up. But she also makes clear that she, like the characters, is caught in the web of desire. She attempts to capture human beings on paper and never entirely succeeds; like the characters themselves, she seeks, desires something she does not find.

The narrator also tells us in the last chapter that Joe and Violet are real: "For me they are real. Sharply in focus and clicking. I wonder, do they know they are the sound of snapping fingers under the sycamores lining the streets?" (226). The reference to music is unmistakable here. The characters are like the notes that the musician plays: the image of desire, caught for a moment "between was and must be" (226), frozen in mid-stride. As the paragraph which follows these words makes clear, it is this clicking that animates the urban world this novel focuses on. But still the narrator confesses that there is something left out: "Something is missing there. Something rogue. Something else you have to figure in before you can figure it out" (228). The sense of indefinable longing and incompleteness, so necessary a part of blues, so clearly a part of this novel, is here the center of the narrative.

Ultimately, this incompleteness takes us back to Joe and Dorcas and their unfinished love. Dorcas's last words are directed to Joe. She tells Felice to tell Joe, "'There's only one apple'" (213). Her statement alludes to Joe's comment to her months before. She asked him to take her to Mexico. After hesitating, then agreeing, he said, "'no point in picking the apple if you don't want to see how it taste'" (40). Both of these statements illustrate the inescapable nature of desire. As Dorcas implies, it is universal: there is only one apple, though we see it in varying guises in this novel. What is more, as Joe implies, there is no flirting with it: one either acts or does not act upon desire. Alice Manfred spends her life denying the power of her dead lover, denying the power of the music she hears. But her desire for him and for the music is still there. Joe acts upon his desire. He eats of the apple. And yet, paradoxically, like Alice Manfred, he finds himself denied the fulfillment he seeks. The allusion to the Adam and Eve story in his statement and Dorcas's statement helps us to understand the elusive nature of fulfillment.

Eve ate of the apple because she was tempted. The snake promised her that such food would give her insight, knowledge, that it would make her like God. In part, the snake is right. Her eyes are opened and so are Adam's. But what Adam and Eve see is the same thing that Morrison's narrator sees, the same thing that Joe sees: that something is missing. They are introduced to death, to the necessity of working for a living. They are led out of the Garden and into the hard reality of the world, a world as harsh and tangible and lively and violent, one might imagine, as the City where Joe and Dorcas live. So Adam and Eve, like all men and women, desire what they do not get. The same applies to Joe and Dorcas. They seek lost parents through their love for one another, and they do not find them. They even seek love in their relationship, and it too evades them. Joe finds out that he does not know how to love, and Dorcas discovers that she really loves Acton. Joe and Dorcas are like Adam and Eve. Their eating of the apple opens their eyes to what they lack, and like every other character in the novel, despite all that they do, they still feel the pain of their orphanhood. We are led to wonder with the narrator what is missing, what may provide completeness. That, of course, is just the message of the blues: there is no completeness, only the story of its absence, whether the characters are Adam and Eve or Joe and Dorcas or Joe and Violet, or whether the story is just the sounds of a saxophone.

Morrison's allusion to Adam and Eve enlarges the dimensions of her story. The fall of humankind is a central myth of Western culture: it presents man and woman as unfulfilled and incomplete. But Morrison uses this allusion to underscore the more pervasive allusions in her novel: those to jazz and blues. Like Adam and Eve, the characters in her song seek what they cannot find. The poignant expression of their aloneness and their estrangement is jazz, a music that is essentially African in form. It makes clear and makes rhythmic the indefinable, unfulfilled nature of all life.

In some respects *Jazz* brings us full circle. The improvisational quality of *The Bluest Eye* emphasized the alienated character of black life. The voice of the primer was so overpowering that no other voice could be heard. Any discussion of black life had to be improvisational because there was no precedent for it. Here quite the reverse is true. Jazz becomes the vehicle for expression, the language of the desires and unrequited longings that are pervasive. It becomes quite literally the rhythm of life. Thus, the tension in this novel is not the same tension that we observed before: the tension between black and white, oral and literate, mainstream culture and African-American culture. Here the tension is a part of life itself: its constant sense of incompleteness. As it does with all other facets of life, jazz makes it rhythmic. So as Bakhtin says of Rabelais, there is for Morrison "no last word," just the rhythm, the ineffable quality of desire. If jazz itself, so poignantly embodied and described in this novel, does not make this clear to the reader, the introductory inscription in the novel does.

Morrison uses inscriptions from the epistles of Paul at the beginning of *Tar Baby* and *Beloved*. At the beginning of *Jazz* she uses a passage from "Thunder, Perfect Mind," a poem from a large body of gnostic writings discovered at Nag Hammadi in 1945:

> I am the name of the sound
> and the sound of the name.
> I am the sign of the letter
> and the designation of the division.

This inscription helps us place this novel in the context of Morrison's other novels, for it suggests to us a world beyond Western thought and a world beyond explanation or logic.

Considered heretical by the early church, the gnostics were quite literally legislated out of existence. According to Elaine Pagels, when Constantine became Christian in the fourth century, the penalty for any kind of heresy could be quite severe, and gnosticism was one of the heresies the church fought with great zeal (xxiii). The very way in which these documents were hidden reveals much about their heretical nature. They were buried in a large earthenware jar near Nag Hammadi sometime around 350 A. D. Clearly, the person who buried them knew of their heretical content, but he or she also considered them sacred. The earthen jar was the standard way to preserve holy but forbidden texts.

But perhaps more important to our understanding of *Jazz* is the nature of gnosticism itself and in particular the nature of this unusual gnostic poem. The Greek word from which gnostic comes is *gnosis*, which literally means knowing. But according to Pagels, the knowing that *gnosis* implies is not rational knowledge. Rather it is insight, the knowledge that allows one to understand the oneness of God and the self (xix). In *Jazz*, we can thus read this inscription as both ironic and forthright. Most of Morrison's characters fail ultimately to find any true self-knowledge, for the narrator concludes finally that something is missing, that desire itself is indefinable. But, by the same token, they do find glimpses; to use Joe's image, they do see the apple and bite into it. So for a moment they find what they seek.

Still, there are other ways to understand this inscription. "Thunder, Perfect Mind" is so unusual that many scholars say it is not gnostic at all. Calling it the "most bizarre of all works from the Nag Hammadi corpus" (38), Bentley Layton states that the poem uses "the rhetorical mode of omnipredication (...) with a logic of antithetical paradox" (38). By this statement Layton implies that the narrator of the poem proclaims herself as that upon which all else is predicated, the source of being. But at the same time, the statements that she makes do not accord with human logic: they are paradoxical and antithetical. The deity who speaks here is clearly female. She has been identified with Isis and with the gnostic goddess Sophia (Mills 916). The particular lines that Morrison uses are significant in that they force the reader to focus upon both music and language. The first two lines refer to sound: "I am the name of the sound/ and the sound of the name." The next two refer to words: "I am the sign of the letter/ and the designation of the division." However, if we look at these lines closely, we find that Layton is correct: their logic unravels. If we apply the first two lines to the word jazz, they lead us nowhere. Jazz is the name of a certain kind of music, but it is also a sound in its own right, a word. The second line is even more puzzling. What is "the sign of the letter" if it is not the letter itself? Further, is "the designation of the division" once again the letter? Does such a phrase imply that we are somehow divided from true knowledge by words themselves? None of these questions can be answered. The "I am" assertions in each of the lines suggest to us a realm beyond the human realm, a deity who is ultimately beyond sound and words. Is this the narrator? Or is it a deity beyond the narrator? Whatever the case, we may safely agree with George MacRae who finds in all the assertions within the poem "the totally other-worldly transcendence of the revealer" (296). Whoever the "revealer" may be, whether the narrator or a female deity, her transcendence is clear.

Such an emphasis upon transcendence is a curious posture for a writer who has consistently played characters, cultures, and points of view against one another, repeatedly suggesting that no one point of view is safe from error and ultimate failure. Indeed, within *Jazz* itself we may safely say that such is the case. Joe's manner of dealing with the ravages of impending old age is no more successful than Violet's. His affair with Dorcas ultimately leaves him in pain just as her longing for a child afflicts her. Everyone in the novel is incomplete, even the narrator herself. Most of the characters hardly know what they seek. So opening with words of "omnipredication" from a female deity contradicts much of what we see in the novel. Still, we must consider the source of the inscription.

These words come to us from a source discredited by Western thought. It is hard to miss the connections to Morrison's career, to jazz itself. Morrison has consistently portrayed a world the West has ignored. Her first novel was the improvised story of a black girl who wanted blue eyes. Her next novel focused upon a lost village where laughter and pain merged, a world that the citizens of Medallion could not even see. In all of these portraits Morrison has undermined traditional explanations, forms, answers—tradition itself. In the process of doing this, she has transformed the very tradition she questions: she makes the hero of the *Bildungsroman* a woman, rewrites the history of slavery, and redefines black and white. It should be little wonder that in *Jazz* she reverses her approach and focuses on music that has redefined American culture by Africanizing it, music that redefines itself even as it is defined by American culture.

So perhaps this is the "loophole" that Bakhtin sees in Rabelais, "a loophole that opens on the distant future and that lends an aspect of ridicule to the relative progressiveness and relative truth accessible to the present or to the immediate future" (*Rabelais* 454). The words of the deity in "Thunder, Perfect Mind" suggest that the world is a big place, that there are voices we in the West have not heard, that there are words and sounds we have no knowledge of, that the very thing we seek is sometimes nebulous and indefinable. Like Adam and Eve, we live in a fallen world. For each of us there is something missing. Like Joe Trace, we see a glimpse of Wild as she disappears into the forest. We hear the music we associate with her. We do not know if she is real, but we do know that we saw something, that we heard something. Like the experience of jazz itself, we can feel it, but we cannot explain it.

Notes

1. Reviewers and critics have observed the importance of music in *Jazz*. Reviewing the novel for *Maclean's*, Diane Turbide states that "the real heart of the story is Harlem itself, alive with possibility and promise" (51). John Leonard, in *The Nation*, notices the importance of improvisation and ties that stylistic feature to the urban setting: "the City,... is itself a kind of jazz improvising its days and nights and blues, its dangerous freedom" (716).

2. In his book *Jazz and the White Americans*, Neil Leonard points out the early connections between blues and jazz. He also enumerates the objections of some middle-class Americans. Among them were these: "it [jazz] affected the brain like alcohol"; "it [jazz] was vulgar and sensual." According to Leonard the most damaging association of jazz "was its identification with the brothel, usually the Negro brothel" (36).

3. Bluebird is well known to this day as a company that records and produces only the finest jazz.

Conclusions

I have argued that the tension in Morrison's work is ultimately the result of the way she defies the expectations of certain members of her audience, specifically those who expect her to be "like Joyce, Hardy, and Faulkner." This tension does not move toward resolution; rather, it is re-invented in each of her novels. But for our purposes, the final re-invention is perhaps more important than any of the others, for in many respects it answers the question with which this study began: that of universality. Morrison's comments to interviewers are in many respects accurate. She does avoid being "like Joyce, Hardy, and Faulkner." She creates a world that by its very being questions the foundations of their worlds. But in creating that world, Morrison includes us all. Thus, it is also true that she does not just address one group or another. Jazz finally becomes for Morrison a universal language of desire. It imposes upon each of us a kind of finitude, for by its very nature it suggests that limitation is a part of each of us. We are limited in what we see. Like Milkman, we fail to understand the complex reality of each life, particularly the lives of those in the shadows: the slave, the wife, the great aunt. We are limited in what we are. Joe Trace discovers that there is always something missing, even when the apple is eaten. All of Morrison's novels function to underscore these points. Still, there is a larger issue at work here: language itself.

Morrison's *Nobel Lecture* underscores the centrality of her conception of language to her work. Using a fable, Morrison sets forth the three components of all novels: a writer, a language, and an audience. An old, blind, wise woman (a writer) is questioned by a group of young people (an audience): is the bird (language) they hold alive or dead? She quickly perceives their power: if she says alive, they will kill the bird; if she says dead, they will let it live. The old woman answers shrewdly that the bird's fate is in the hands of the questioners, imagining the ways in which it (language) may die. What she imagines is quite literally a catalog of all of those fatal constraints that destroy the life of a language, that make it into what she calls "unyielding language" (13).

Morrison includes in this category many types of language: "statist language," "official language," "faux language of the mindless media," "the proud but calcified language of the academy," and "the commodity-driven language of science" (13-16). She expresses the characteristic they all share in one densely packed sentence: "Unreceptive to interrogation, it [the unyielding language] cannot form or tolerate new ideas, shape other thoughts, tell another story, fill baffling silences" (14). In short, language dies whenever writer and reader finalize it, when one utterance becomes the perfect word, the official thought, the final story of any given experience. Lincoln's speech at Gettysburg becomes for Morrison a model of living language because it avoids what Morrison calls "the 'final word,' the precise 'summing up'" (20). Lincoln acknowledges what Morrison acknowledges in *Jazz*: the fact that "language can never live up to life once and for all" (21). It can never fully explain or embody grief or sacrifice or any other complex human emotion. It is part of our finitude. And yet paradoxically, it becomes a part of our gesture toward what Morrison calls "the ineffable."

Perhaps it is that very perception that makes it inevitable that there will always be another story, another word. In fact, that is just what the other part of this triangle demands. The young people questioning the old woman do not want to be told that they hold language in their hands. They are holding nothing. Furthermore, all they want is another story, a story that will enable them "to see without pictures." For they know what we all do: that, in Morrison's words, "language alone protects us from the scariness of things with no name" (28). So it must have been for Morrison herself at the beginning of her writing career. It was the namelessness of black experience which gave birth to *The Bluest Eye*. The very inarticulation of the narrator of that novel suggests to us the enormity (the "scariness") of what the primer does not say. The primer, after all, proclaims itself to be that final word, that summing up of all family experience. Claudia must tell her story in its shadow, seeking a form for the enormity of her experience. In a sense all of Morrison's later novels do what Claudia does in *The Bluest Eye*. They interrogate that which proclaims itself "unreceptive to interrogation": the *Bildungsroman*, the history of slavery, the very foundation of the social order in this country. In fact, in every novel there is the same question that Claudia confronts: finding a form for the enormity of experience, knowing all the while that "language can never live up to life" (21). Still, there is that need for one more story, one more word, one more attempt to reach the ineffable.

In his last article Bakhtin enlarged the meaning of the term dialogue:

> There is neither a first word nor a last word. The contexts of dialogue are without limit. They extend into the deepest past and the most distant future. Even meanings born in dialogues of the remotest past will never be fully grasped once and for all, for they will always be renewed in later dialogue. (Clark and Holquist 348 - 350)

Morrison's work in many ways embodies Bakhtin's contention that there is no "last word." In fact, to the degree that she rejects comparisons between her work and that of more traditional writers such as Joyce, Hardy, and Faulkner, she insists that the dialogue continue, that we as readers respond to new forms, new ideas, new characters. But her work is more than mere response. Morrison refuses to follow predictable patterns within her own work because such patterns presuppose a "last word," a resolution. Rather she re-invents her alienation in each novel, making us aware of an unfinished world, both inside of us and outside of us, much bigger than any of us might have imagined.

Works Cited

Angelo, Bonnie. "The Pain of Being Black: An Interview with Toni Morrison." *Conversations with Toni Morrison.* Ed. Danille Taylor-Guthrie. Jackson: University Press of Mississippi, 1994. 255-261.

Awkward, Michael. *Inspiriting Influences: Tradition, Revision, and Afro-American Women's Novels.* New York: Columbia, 1989.

———. "'Unruly and Let Loose': Myth, Ideology, and Gender in *Song of Solomon.*" *Callaloo* 13 (Summer, 1990): 482-498.

———. "Roadblocks and Relatives: Critical Revision in Toni Morrison's *The Bluest Eye.*" *Critical Essays on Toni Morrison.* Ed. Nellie McKay. Boston: G.K. Hall, 1988. 57-68.

Bakerman, Susan. "The Seams Can't Show: An Interview with Toni Morrison." *Black American Literature Forum* 12 (1978): 56-60.

Bakhtin, M. M. *The Dialogic Imagination.* Ed. Michael Holquist. Translated by Michael Holquist and Caryl Emerson. Austin: The University of Texas Press, 1981.

———. *Rabelais and his World.* Trans. Helene Iswolsky. Bloomington: Indiana University Press, 1984.

Barlowe, Arthur. "Arthur Barlowe's Narrative of the 1584 Voyage." *The First Colonist.* Ed. David B. Quinn and Alison M. Quinn. Raliegh: North Carolina Department of Cultural Resources, 1982. 1-12.

Bell, Bernard. *The Afro-American Novel and Its Tradition.* Amherst: The University of Massachusetts Press, 1987.

Bloom, Harold, Ed. *Modern Critical Views: Toni Morrison.* New York: Chelsea, 1990.

Broad, Robert L. "Giving Blood to the Scraps: Haints, History, and Hosea in *Beloved.*" *African-American Review* 28 (1994): 189-196.

Brenner, Gerry. "*Song of Solomon*: Rejecting Rank's Monomyth and Feminism." *Critical Essays on Toni Morrison.* Ed. Nellie McKay. Boston: G.K. Hall, 1988. 114-125.

Bruck, Peter. "Returning to One's Roots: The Motif of Searching and Flying in Toni Morrison's *Song of Solomon.*" *The Afro-American Novel Since 1960.* Ed. Peter Bruck and Wolfgang Karrer. Amsterdam: Gruner, 1982. 289-305.

Butler-Evans, Elliott. *Race, Gender, and Desire: Narrative Strategies in the Fiction of Toni Cade Bambara, Toni Morrison, and Alice Walker.* Philadelphia: Temple University Press, 1989.

Byerman, Keith. *Fingering the Jagged Grain: Tradition and Form in Recent Black Fiction.* Athens: University of Georgia Press, 1985.

———. "Beyond Realism: The Fiction of Toni Morrison." *Toni Morrison.* Ed. Harold Bloom. NewYork: Chelsea, 1990. 55-84.

Campbell, Joseph. *The Hero with a Thousand Faces.* Second Edition. Bollingen Series XVII. Princeton, New Jersey: Princeton, 1973.

Chase, Richard. *The American Novel and Its Tradition.* Garden City, New York: Doubleday, 1957.

Clark, Katarina and Michael Holquist. *Mikhail Bakhtin.* Cambridge: Harvard, 1984.

Conrad, Joseph. "The Secret Sharer." *The Portable Conrad.* Revised Edition. Ed. Morton Dauwen Zabel. New York: Viking, 1975. 650-699.

Cowart, David. "Faulkner and Joyce in Morrison's *Song of Solomon. American Literature* 62 (March 1990): 87-100.

Davis, Cynthia. "Self, Society, and Myth in Toni Morrison's Fiction." *Modern Critical Views: Toni Morrison.* New York: Chelsea House, 1990. 7-25.

de Weaver, Jacqueline. "The Inverted World of Toni Morrison's *Sula." College Language Association Journal* 4 (1979): 402 - 414.

Douglass, Frederick. *Narrative of the Life of Frederick Douglass. Frederick Douglass: The Narrative and Selected Writings.* Ed. Michael Meyer. New York: The Modern Library, 1984.

Eliot, T. S. *The Complete Poems and Plays: 1909-1950.* New York: Harcourt, Brace and World, 1971.

Fiedler, Leslie A. *Love and Death in the American Novel.* Revised Edition. New York: Stein and Day, 1966.

Fox-Genovese, Elizabeth. "Of Quilts and Cape Jasmines: Elements of Common Southern Culture." *Humanities in the South* 75 (Spring 1992): 1-4.

Gates, Henry Louis, Jr. *Figures in Black: Word, Signs, and the Racial Self.* Oxford: Oxford University Press, 1987

———. *The Signifying Monkey.* New York: Oxford, 1988.

Grant, Robert, "Absence into Presence: The Thematics of Memory 'Missing' Subjects in Toni Morrison's *Sula." Essays on Toni Morrison.* Ed. Nellie McKay. Boston: G. K. Hall, 1988. 90-105.

Gray, Paul. Book Review of *Jazz. Time* 27 April 1992: 70.

Hamilton, Edith. *Mythology*. Boston: Little, Brown, and Company, 1942.

Harris, Trudier. *Fiction and Folklore: The Novels of Toni Morri son*. Knoxville: The University of Tennessee Press, 1991.

———. "Reconnecting Fragments: Afro-American Folk Tradition in *The Bluest Eye*." *Critical Essays on Toni Morrison*. Ed. Nellie McKay. Boston: G.K. Hall, 1988. 68-76.

Harris, Norman. "The Black Universe in Contemporary Afro-American Fiction." *College Language Association Journal* 30 (September, 1986): 1-13.

Hedin, Raymond. "Strategies of Form in the American Slave Narrative." *Essays in Criticism and Theory*. Ed. John Sekora and Darwin Turner. Macomb: Western Illinios University Press, 1982. 25-35.

Hemenway, Robert. "In the American Canon." *Redefining American Literary History*. Eds. A. LaVonne Brown Ruoff and Jerry W. Ward, Jr. New York: MLA, 1990. 62-75.

Henderson, Mae Gwendolyn. "Speaking in Tongues: Dialogics, Dialectics, and the Black Woman Writer's Literary Tradition." *Changing Our Own Words*. Ed. Cheryl Wall. New Brunswick: Rutgers, 1989. 16-35.

Hilfer, Anthony C. "Critical Indeterminacies in Toni Morrison's Fiction." *Texas Studies in Literature and Language* 33 (Spring 1991): 91-95.

Holloway, Karla F. C. and Stephanie Demetrakopoulos. *New Dimensions of Spirituality: A Biracial and Bicultural Reading of the Novels of Toni Morrison*. New York: Greenwood, 1987.

Horn, Miriam. "Five Years of Terror." *U.S. News and World Report*. 19 October 1987: 75.

House, Elizabeth. "Artists and the Art of Living: Order and Disorder in Toni Morrison's Fiction. "*Modern Fiction* Studies 34 (Spring 1988): 27-44.

Hovet, Grace Ann and Barbara Lounsberry. "Flying as Symbol and Legend in Toni Morrison's *The Bluest Eye, Sula,* and *Song of Solomon." College Language Association Journal* 27 (December, 1983): 119-140.

Jones, Bessie W. and Audrey L. Vinson. *The World of Toni Morrison.* Dubuque, Iowa: Kendall Hunt, 1985.

Kolodony, Annette. "Dancing Through the Minefield." *Feminist Criticism: Essays on Women, Literature, and Theory.* Ed. Elaine Showalter. New York: Pantheon, 1985. 145-168.

Layton, Bentley. *The Gnostic Scriptures.* New York: Doubleday, 1987.

———. "The Riddle of the Thunder (NHC VI, 2): The Function of Paradox in a Gnostic Text from Nag Hammadi." *Nag Hammadi, Gnosticism, and Early Christianity.* Ed. Charles W. Hedrick and Robert Hodgson, Jr. Peabody, Massachu setts: Hendrickson, 1986.

Lee, Dorothy H. "The Quest for Self: Triumph and Failure in the Works of Toni Morrison." *Black Women Writers (1950 -1980): A Critical Evaluation.* Ed. Mari Evans. New York: Doubleday, 1984. 346-360.

Leonard, Neil. *Jazz and the White Americans: The Acceptance of a New Art Form.* Chicago: The University of Chicago Press, 1962.

Leonard, John. "Her Soul's High Song." *The Nation* 25 May 1992: 706-718.

Lester, Rosemarie K. "An Interview with Toni Morrison." *Critical Essays on Toni Morrison.* Ed. Nellie McKay. Boston: G. K. Hall, 1988. 47-54.

MaCrae, George W. Introduction to "The Thunder: Perfect Mind (VI, 2)." *The Nag Hammadi Library.* Ed. John M. Robiso n. Revised Edition. San Francisco: Harper, 1990. 294-298.

Marshall, Brenda. "The Gospel According to Pilate." *American Literature* 57 (October, 1985): 486-489.

Marx, Leo. *The Machine in the Garden: Technology and the Pastoral Ideal in American Literature*. New York: Oxford, 1972.

Mbalia, Dorothea D. *Toni Morrison's Developing Class Consciousness*. Selinsgrove: Susquehanna University Press, 1991.

McDowell, Deborah E. "Reading Toni Morrison's *Sula* and the Black Female Text." *Modern Critical Views: Toni Morrison*. Ed. Harold Bloom. New York: Chelsea House, 1990. 149-163.

McKay, Nellie, ed. *Critical Essays on Toni Morrison*. Boston: G.K. Hall, 1988.

Mills, Watson E. General Editor. *Mercer Dictionary of the Bible*. Macon, Georgia: Mercer University Press, 1990.

Mobley, Marilyn Sanders. *Folk Roots and Mythic Wings in Sarah Orne Jewett and Toni Morrison: The Cultural Function of Narrative*. Baton Rouge: LSU, 1991.

Morrison, Toni. *Beloved*. New York: Knopf, 1987.

———. *The Bluest Eye*. New York: Washington, Square, 1972.

———. *Jazz*. New York: Alfred A. Knopf, 1992.

———. *The Nobel Lecture in Literature, 1993*. New York: Knopf, 1994.

———. *Playing in the Dark: Whiteness and the Literary Imagination*. Cambridge: Harvard, 1992.

———. *Song of Solomon*. New York: Knopf, 1977.

———. *Sula*. New York: Knopf, 1973.

———. *Tar Baby*. New York: Knopf, 1981.

———. "Unspeakable Things Unspoken: The Afro-American Presence in American Literature. *Modern Critical Views: Toni Morrison*. Ed. Harold Bloom. New York: Chelsea, 1990. 201-230.

Neil, William. *Harper's Bible Commentary*. New York: Harper, 1962.

O'Brien, Edna. Book Review of *Jazz*. *New York Times Book Review*. 5 April 1992: 1.

Otten, Terry. *The Crime of Innocence in the Fiction of Toni Morrison*. Columbia: The University of Missouri Press, 1989.

Oxford English Dictionary (OED). Second Edition. 20 vols. Oxford: Clarendon Press, 1989.

Pagels, Elaine. *The Gnostic Gospels*. New York: Random House, 1979.

Payne, Robert. *Ancient Rome*. New York: American Heritage, 1970.

Rigney, Barbara Hill. *The Voices of Toni Morrison*. Columbus: Ohio State University Press, 1991

Roberts, John W. "The African-American Animal Trickster as Hero." *Redefining American Literary History*. Eds. A. LaVonne Brown Ruoff and Jerry W. Ward, Jr. New York: MLA, 1990. 97-115.

Royster, Philip. "Milkman's Flying: The Scapegoat Transcendedin Toni Morrison's *Song of Solomon*." *College Language Association Journal* 4 (June 1981): 419-440.

Russell, Sandi. "It's OK to say OK: An Interview Essay." *Critical Essays on Toni Morrison*. Ed. Nellie McKay. Boston: G.K. Hall, 1988. 43-47.

Samuels, Wilfred and Clenora Hudson. *Toni Morrison*. Boston: Twayne, 1990.

Schuller, Gunther. *Early Jazz: Its Roots and Musical Development*. New York: Oxford, 1968.

Schmudde, Carol E. "The Haunting of 124." *African American Review* 26 (1992): 409 - 416.

Schwartz, Amy E. "'Beloved': It's not a Question of Who Suffered More." *The Washington Post*. April 13, 1988: B7.

Sekora, John. "Comprehending Slavery: Language and Personal History in the *Narrative*." *Modern Ciritical Interpretations:*

Narrative of the Life of Frederick Douglass. Ed. Harold Bloom. New York: Chelsea House, 1988. 149-161.

Smith, Valerie. *Self-Discovery and Authority in Afro-American Narrative.* Cambridge: Harvard, 1987.

Stein, Karen F. "Toni Morrison's *Sula*: A Black Woman's Epic." *Black American Literature Forum* 18 (Winter 1984): 146-150.

Stryz, Jan. "Inscribing an Origin in *Song of Solomon.*" *Studies in American Fiction* 19.1 (Spring 1991): 31-40.

Tate, Claudia. Interview with Toni Morrison. *Black Women Writers at Work.* New York: Continuum, 1983. 117-131.

The Bible. The King James Version. New York: American Bible Society, 1962.

Tirrell, Lynne. "Storytelling and Moral Agency." *The Journal of Aesthetics and Art Criticism* 48 (Spring 1990) : 112 -115.

Tirro, Frank. *Jazz: A History.* New York: Norton, 1977.

Turbide, Diane. "Taking the A Train (Book Review of *Jazz*)." *Macleans.* June 1992: 51.

Ulanov, Barry. *A History of Jazz in America.* New York: Da Capo Press, 1972.

Wagner, Linda. "Mastery of Narrative." *Contemporary American Women Writers.* Eds. Catharine Rainwater and William J. Scheick. Lexington: The University Press of Kentucky, 1985. 197-207.

Wegs, Joyce M. "Toni Morrison's *Song of Solomon*: A Blues Song." *Essays in Literature* 9 (Fall, 1982): 211-223.

Willis, Susan. "Eruptions of Funk: Historicizing Toni Morrison." *Black American Literature Forum* 16 (1982):34-42.

Wolff, Cynthia Griffin. "'Margaret Garner': A Cincinnati Story." *The Massachusetts Review* 32 (Fall, 1991): 417-440.

Wong, Shelley. "Transgression as Poesis in *The Bluest Eye.*" *Callaloo.* 13(1990): 471-481.

Wright, Richard. *Native Son.* New York: Harper, 1940.

Index

The 121
Pagels, Elaine 133
Paul, The Apostle 96, 97, 115, 116
Perseus 56
Playing in the Dark 9, 14, 15, 34, 51, 71, 72, 79, 84
Rabelais and his World 45, 120
Rabelais, FranÇois 45, 120, 133, 136
Rainey, Ma 126
Rank, Otto 56
rhetoric 30, 120
Rigney, Barbara Hill 13, 14, 55, 56
Roberts, John 90
Romulus 56
Royster, Philip 38
Russell, Sandi 2
Samuels, Wilfred D. 2, 11, 38
Scapegoat 38
Schuller, Gunther 121, 127, 128
Schwartz, Amy 104
"Secret Sharer, The" 80, 82, 83
Sekora, John 102, 108,
signifying 7, 60, 93, 94
Sir Gawain and the Green Knight 60
Slave Narrative 21, 102-105, 107, 110
slavery 15, 51, 101-103, 106-110, 112, 114, 116, 136, 141
Smith, Bessie 126
Smith, Valerie 38
Song of Solomon 4, 11, 20, 55-57, 62, 64, 67, 73, 74, 77,78, 84, 94, 96, 97, 111
Stacy, Jess 123
Stein, Karen 38
Stryz, Jan 4, 5
Sula 4, 20, 37-44, 46, 49-52, 55, 56, 62, 77, 78, 84
Tar Baby 11, 77-79, 82-84, 87-94, 96, 119, 133
Tate, Claudia 2, 3, 41
Temple, Shirley 32
Their Eyes Were Watching God 7
Thoreau, Henry David 15, 59
"Thunder, Perfect Mind" 133-136
Tiresias 31, 35
Tirrell, Lynne 24
Tocqueville, Alexis de 34
Toomer, Jean 6, 7, 57